# Mechanics, Grammar, & Usage
## Grades 4-5

> Turn to each section to find a more detailed skills list.

## Table of Contents

## What Does This Book Include?

- More than 75 student practice pages that reinforce basic mechanics, grammar, and usage skills
- A detailed skills list for each section of the book
- Send-home letters that inform parents of the skills being targeted and ways to practice these skills
- Student checkups
- A reproducible student progress chart
- Awards to celebrate student progress
- Answer keys for easy checking
- Perforated pages for easy removal and filing if desired

## What Are the Benefits of This Book?

- Organized for quick and easy use
- Enhances and supports your existing reading and writing programs
- Offers multiple practice opportunities
- Helps develop mastery of basic skills
- Provides reinforcement for different ability levels
- Includes communication pages that encourage parents' participation in their children's learning of reading and writing
- Contains checkups that assess students' mechanics, grammar, and usage knowledge
- Offers a reproducible chart for documenting student progress
- Aligns with national literacy standards

# How to Use This Book
## Steps to Success

## Choose Skills to Target

Scan the detailed table of contents at the beginning of each section to find just the right skills to target your students' needs.

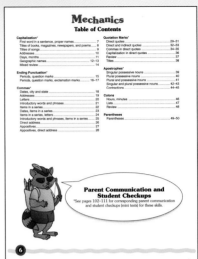

## Select Fun Practice Pages

Choose from a variety of fun formats the pages that best match your students' current ability levels.

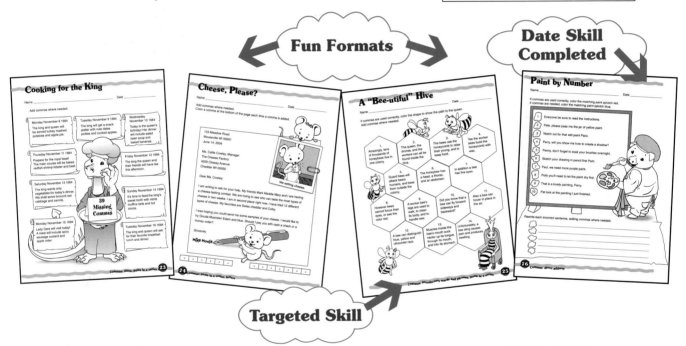

**Fun Formats**

**Date Skill Completed**

**Targeted Skill**

**Letter to Parents Informing Them of Skill to Review**

**Problems for Practice**

**Skills Review for Parents**

## Communicate With Parents

Recruit parent assistance by locating the appropriate parent letter (pages 102–122), making copies, and sending the letter home.

# Assess Student Understanding

Assess students' progress with student checkups (mini tests) on pages 103–123. Choose Checkup A or Checkup B.

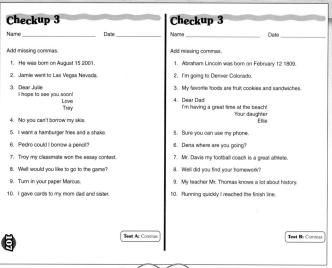

**Checkup 3**

Name _____ Date _____

Add missing commas.

1. He was born on August 15 2001.
2. Jamie went to Las Vegas Nevada.
3. Dear Julie
   I hope to see you soon!
   Love
   Trey
4. No you can't borrow my skis.
5. I want a hamburger fries and a shake.
6. Pedro could I borrow a pencil?
7. Troy my classmate won the essay contest.
8. Well would you like to go to the game?
9. Turn in your paper Marcus.
10. I gave cards to my mom dad and sister.

**Test A:** Commas

**Checkup 3**

Name _____ Date _____

Add missing commas.

1. Abraham Lincoln was born on February 12 1809.
2. I'm going to Denver Colorado.
3. My favorite foods are fruit cookies and sandwiches.
4. Dear Dad
   I'm having a great time at the beach!
   Your daughter
   Ellie
5. Sure you can use my phone.
6. Dena where are you going?
7. Mr. Davis my football coach is a great athlete.
8. Well did you find your homework?
9. My teacher Mr. Thomas knows a lot about history.
10. Running quickly I reached the finish line.

**Test B:** Commas

Two Checkups for Each Skill

# Document Progress

Documenting student progress can be as easy as 1, 2, 3! Do the following for each student:

1. Make a copy of the Student Progress Chart (page 101).
2. File the chart in his portfolio or a class notebook.
3. Record the date each checkup is given, the number of correct answers, and any comments regarding his progress.

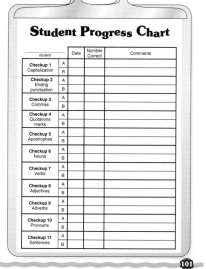

**Student Progress Chart**

| student | | Date | Number Correct | Comments |
|---|---|---|---|---|
| Checkup 1 Capitalization | A | | | |
| | B | | | |
| Checkup 2 Ending punctuation | A | | | |
| | B | | | |
| Checkup 3 Commas | A | | | |
| | B | | | |
| Checkup 4 Quotations marks | A | | | |
| | B | | | |
| Checkup 5 Apostrophes | A | | | |
| | B | | | |
| Checkup 6 Nouns | A | | | |
| | B | | | |
| Checkup 7 Verbs | A | | | |
| | B | | | |
| Checkup 8 Adjectives | A | | | |
| | B | | | |
| Checkup 9 Adverbs | A | | | |
| | B | | | |
| Checkup 10 Pronouns | A | | | |
| | B | | | |
| Checkup 11 Sentences | A | | | |
| | B | | | |

101

# Celebrate!

Celebrate mechanics, grammar, and usage success using the awards on page 124.

Great aim!

_____
student

is right on target with

_____
skill

_____
teacher

_____
date

You hit the bull's-eye!

_____
student

hit the mark with

_____
skill

_____
teacher

_____
date

## Books in the Target Reading & Writing Success Series:

- *Mechanics, Grammar, & Usage* • Grs. 2–3
- *Mechanics, Grammar, & Usage* • Grs. 4–5
- *Word Skills & Vocabulary* • Grs. 2–3
- *Word Skills & Vocabulary* • Grs. 4–5

**Managing Editor:** Debra Liverman

**Editorial Team:** Becky S. Andrews, Kimberley Bruck, Karen P. Shelton, Diane Badden, Cayce Guiliano, Debra Liverman, Lauren E. Cox, Peggy W. Hambright, Sherry McGregor, Karen A. Brudnak, Sarah Hamblet, Hope Rodgers, Dorothy C. McKinney, Kim Minafo, Cindy Mondello

**Production Team:** Lisa K. Pitts, Pam Crane, Clevell Harris, Rebecca Saunders, Jennifer Tipton Bennett, Chris Curry, Theresa Lewis Goode, Ivy L. Koonce, Clint Moore, Greg D. Rieves, Barry Slate, Donna K. Teal, Tazmen Carlisle, Amy Kirtley-Hill, Kristy Parton, Debbie Shoffner, Cathy Edwards Simrell, Lynette Dickerson, Mark Rainey

# www.themailbox.com

©2004 by THE EDUCATION CENTER, INC.
All rights reserved.
ISBN# 1-56234-614-8

Mechanics

5

# Mechanics
## Table of Contents

## Parent Communication and Student Checkups

*See pages 102–111 for corresponding parent communication and student checkups (mini tests) for these skills.

# Snakes Alive!

Name _____ Date _____

If the snake section has a capitalization mistake, color it yellow.
If the snake section has correct capitalization, color it green.

1. | anna conda | loves living | in the | jungle. |

2. | She | and | bennie boa | are | best friends. |

3. | the two friends | crawl along | the riverbank | and talk. |

4. | anna loves to watch | mickey monkey | swing from the | branches. |

5. | mr. monkey's | kids | are afraid | of anna. |

6. | it's no | wonder | the children | are scared! |

7. | did you | know | anna can | grow to be | 30 feet long? |

8. | She is | the longest | snake in her | village. |

9. | even though | she sometimes | bites, | anna is not | poisonous. |

10. | her | teeth can | cause | bad | wounds though. |

11. | when she | gets hungry, | anna wraps | herself tightly | around her | dinner. |

12. | that's the | time to | stay out of | anna's way! |

Capitalization: first word in a sentence, proper names

# Out-of-This-World Reading!

Name _____     Date _____

Write each title with correct capitalization.

**Books**
- (L) 1. one flew over the moon
- (S) 2. the view from venus
- (S) 3. a star is born
- (G) 4. the man in the moon

Remember to underline the titles of books, magazines, and newspapers and use quotation marks around titles of poems.

**Newspapers**
- (E) 5. galaxy gazette
- (T) 6. the daily star
- (T) 7. the space observer
- (I) 8. the milky way press

_____
_____
_____
_____

**Poems**
- (S) 9. "twinkling star"
- (L) 10. "the outer limits of space"
- (H) 11. "stargazing"

**Magazines**
- (E) 12. space quest
- (U) 13. mars life
- (A) 14. eyes on space

_____
_____
_____

## How do aliens read at night?

To solve the riddle, match the letters in parentheses to the numbered lines below.

They __ __ __  " __ __ __ __ __  —  __ __ __ __ __ __ " !
    13 9 5   2 14 6 12 10   1 8 4 11 7 3

# "Meow-velous" Masterpieces

Name _____     Date _____

Write each song title with correct capitalization.

1. black cat strut
_____
_____
_____

2. the year of the cat
_____
_____
_____

3. the cat from outer space
_____
_____
_____

4. wake up, wildcats!
_____
_____
_____

5. a dream of a thousand cats
_____
_____
_____

6. frisky whiskers
_____
_____
_____

7. come here, my kitty
_____
_____
_____

8. at the scratching post
_____
_____
_____

Make up a song title for each description.
Write your titles using correct capitalization.

9. a new cat at school
_____
_____
_____

10. a fight between two cats
_____
_____
_____

11. newborn kittens
_____
_____
_____

Remember to use quotation marks around titles of songs.

12. strong cats
_____
_____

13. the most popular cats in school
_____
_____

# Birthday-Bunny Blues

Name _____ Date _____

Circle the letters that should be capitalized.
Write the address using correct capitalization.

**Return to Sender**
Bun E. rabbit
62 barn house Trail
hareville, KY 20948

1.

**Return to Sender**
ima Hare
136 Carrot place
Rabbit run, TX 58392

2.

**Return to Sender**
Fur e. Friend
2800 wabbit Way
Bunny hop, MA 38582

3.

**Return to Sender**
pete R. Rabbit
39 Hoppers road
Furville, nc 28764

4.

**Return to Sender**
farmer Brown
746 Barnyard lane
hopping, SC 04952

5.

**Return to Sender**
Flop see
291 rabbit hole Court
cotton Tail, Tn 62522

6.

# Doctor's Orders

Name _____    Date _____

If capital letters are used correctly, color the letter in the "Correct" column.

If capital letters are needed, color the letter in the "Incorrect" column.

Then circle the letters that should be capitalized.

| | Correct | Incorrect |
|---|---|---|
| 1. Dr. Woof sees patients on monday, tuesday, and Thursday. | E | A |
| 2. The doctor makes rounds at St. Bernard Hospital on Wednesday and friday. | K | P |
| 3. Lane the Great Dane will have a checkup the last Friday in march. | L | S |
| 4. Sally Spaniel will come back in december to get her cast off. | M | D |
| 5. If Max Mutt is not well by Monday, Dr. Woof will put him in the hospital. | O | S |
| 6. Dr. Woof has seen 49 cats since Monday. | H | G |
| 7. Bobby Boxer visits the doctor every Thursday for a blood test. | E | C |
| 8. Dr. Woof is taking the month of June off to visit his family. | M | H |
| 9. Bonnie Beagle will need to take her medicine through next sunday. | B | O |
| 10. Dr. Woof plays catch with his doctor friends on saturdays. | F | L |
| 11. Tim Terrier will have surgery on the first tuesday in May. | A | S |
| 12. Dr. Woof will check him the next Friday. | O | T |

## What did Dr. Woof tell Polly Poodle to use for her rash?

To solve the riddle, match the colored letters to the numbered lines below.

" __ __ __ __ - __ __ __ __ __ __ "
 11 6  1  8     2  9  5  4  10 7

# Find the Fort!

Name _____ Date _____

Circle the letters that should be capitalized.
Connect the words with circled letters to lead Rascal to the fort.

**Start**

coast    mexico    latitude

north america    pacific ocean    rocky mountains

ocean

new york    climate    great lakes

island    mississippi river

equator    south carolina

harbor    atlantic ocean    continent    grand canyon

beach    desert    mesa

inlet

oregon trail

california

gulf of mexico

volcano    louisiana    canada    kansas    erie canal    death valley

valley    hawaii

alaska    river    **Finish**

# The Big Apple

Name _____    Date _____

Circle the letters that should be capitalized.
The number tells how many letters should be circled.

1. The largest city in the united states is new york city, sometimes called the Big Apple. (5)

2. Many people move to the city from puerto rico, china, central america, and the caribbean islands. (7)

3. The Statue of Liberty stands on liberty island in new york harbor. (5)

4. New york city is divided into five boroughs: manhattan, the bronx, queens, brooklyn, and staten island. (8)

5. Manhattan is surrounded by the hudson river, the east river, the harlem river, and upper new york bay. (10)

6. One famous sight in new york city is the 102-story Empire State Building. (3)

7. The World Trade Center's twin 110-story towers were once the tallest skyscrapers on manhattan island. (2)

Capitalization: geographic names

# Bunking for the Night

Name _____   Date _____

Color each stone that contains a proper noun (or nouns) that should be capitalized.

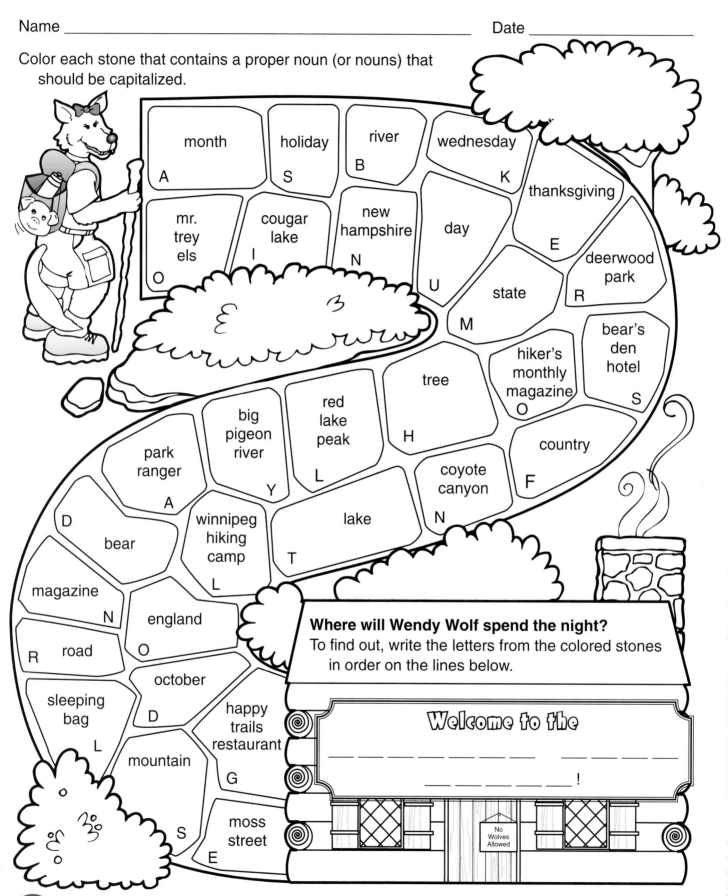

month
A

holiday
S

river
B

wednesday
K

thanksgiving
E

mr. trey els
O

cougar lake
I

new hampshire
N

day
U

deerwood park
R

state
M

bear's den hotel
S

hiker's monthly magazine
O

tree
H

big pigeon river
Y

red lake peak
L

country
F

park ranger
A

winnipeg hiking camp
L

lake
T

coyote canyon
N

bear
D

magazine
N

england
O

road
R

october
D

sleeping bag
L

mountain

happy trails restaurant
G

moss street
E

**Where will Wendy Wolf spend the night?**
To find out, write the letters from the colored stones in order on the lines below.

Welcome to the

____ ____ ____ ____ ____ ____ ____ ____ ____

____ ____ ____ ____ ____ ____ ____ !

No Wolves Allowed

©The Education Center, Inc. • *Target Reading & Writing Success* • TEC60875 • Key p. 126

*Capitalization: mixed review*

# Daydreamers?

Name _____ Date _____

Color the part of the tail with the correct ending punctuation.

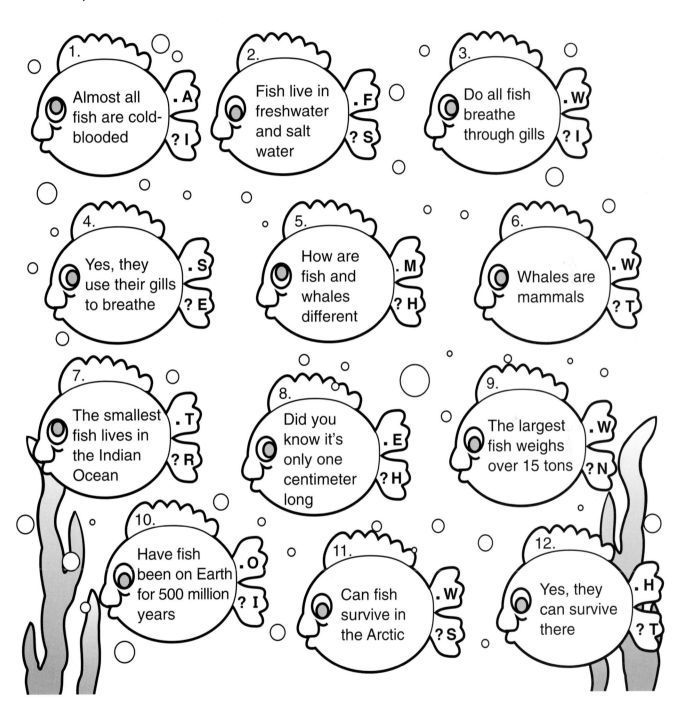

1. Almost all fish are cold-blooded  . A  ? I
2. Fish live in freshwater and salt water  . F  ? S
3. Do all fish breathe through gills  . W  ? I
4. Yes, they use their gills to breathe  . S  ? E
5. How are fish and whales different  . M  ? H
6. Whales are mammals  . W  ? T
7. The smallest fish lives in the Indian Ocean  . T  ? R
8. Did you know it's only one centimeter long  . E  ? H
9. The largest fish weighs over 15 tons  . W  ? N
10. Have fish been on Earth for 500 million years  . O  ? I
11. Can fish survive in the Arctic  . W  ? S
12. Yes, they can survive there  . H  ? T

## What do you call a scaly creature with a dream?
To solve the riddle, write the shaded letters in order on the lines.

__ __ __ __ __ __ __   __ I __ __   A __ __ __ __ !

**Ending punctuation: periods, question marks**

# Searching High and Low

Name _____ Date _____

Write the correct ending punctuation mark in each acorn.

1. Sam, what are you doing ◯

2. I'm looking for all the food I stored last fall ◯
   I'm really hungry ◯

3. Do you remember where you hid it ◯

4. Well, I think I hid it near a pile of leaves ◯ I just can't
   remember which one ◯

5. Do you want some help ◯

6. That would be great ◯ Maybe if we both look we can
   find it ◯

7. Okay ◯ I'll check these leaves near your nest ◯

8. I'll look over here by these bushes ◯

9. Do you see anything ◯

10. Not yet, but I'll keep looking ◯

11. I can hear my stomach growling ◯ I hope we find it quickly ◯

12. Hey, Sam, I found your food ◯

13. Where was it ◯

14. It was right under your nose ◯
    It's in the leaves by your nest ◯

**Ending punctuation: periods, question marks, exclamation marks**

# Monkeys at the Movies

Name _____  Date _____

Add the correct ending punctuation marks.
After you add a mark, color a matching piece of popcorn.

1. Which movie do you want to see

2. Let's get tickets for *Going Bananas*

3. Do you want some popcorn or candy

4. I want some popcorn and a soda

5. Here are the snacks

6. Hurry up because the movie is starting

7. Wow, this movie is fantastic

8. I really like it too

9. That jungle scene was awesome

10. What do you think will happen next

11. I think the monkey will chase the Banana Bandit

12. Who will get the bananas in the end

13. We'll just have to wait and see

14. I love going to the movies

period

exclamation mark

question mark

Ending punctuation: periods, question marks, exclamation marks

# Ellie's Explorations

Name _____    Date _____

**PASSPORT**

Name: Ellie Elephant

Boise
3-26-1988
Idaho

Dallas
5-17-1987
Texas

Harrisburg
4-9-1990
Pennsylvania

Seattle
6-23-1993
Washington

Miami
4-21-1984
Florida

Boston
10-8-2000
Massachusetts

Chicago
7-15-1998
Illinois

Phoenix
2-18-2003
Arizona

Bangor
12-28-2001
Maine

Baltimore
4-3-2004
Maryland

Write each date and location of Ellie's travels.
Add commas where needed.
The first one has been done for you.

| **Location** | | **Date** |
|---|---|---|
| *Boise, Idaho* | on | *March 26, 1988* |
| _____ | on | _____ |
| _____ | on | _____ |
| _____ | on | _____ |
| _____ | on | _____ |
| _____ | on | _____ |
| _____ | on | _____ |
| _____ | on | _____ |
| _____ | on | _____ |
| _____ | on | _____ |

**Commas: dates, city and state**

# A "Bear-y" Wild Party

Name _____ Date _____

If commas are used correctly, color the paw.
Cross out commas that are not used correctly.
Add commas where needed.

## Guest List

(B) Ima Bear
32 Shaggy Lane
New Orleans LA, 70112

(L) Grizzly Bear
142 Hibernating Lane
New York NY 10001

(K) Wanna B. A. Bear
483 Rocky Mountain Road
Boise, ID 83701

(U) Bear E. Scary
947 Yellowstone Road
Jackson, Hole WY 83001

(M) Brown Bear
183 Hill Road
High Point, NC 27265

(E) Black E. Bear
P.O. Box 674
Grand, Canyon AZ 86023

(B) Poll R. Bear
P.O. Box 743
Nome AK 99762

(E) Bay B. Bear
681 Furry Lane
New, Bedford MA 02740

(S) Brown E. Bear
574 Cave Court
St. Paul, MN 55101

(A) Fuzzy Bear
283 Growling Lane
Lake Placid NY 12946

(R) Furry Bear
563 Claw Court
Fort Lauderdale FL, 33301

(Y) Q. T. Bear
3526 Tree Lane
Libby MT 59923

## What kind of pie will be served at Bear's party?

To solve the riddle, write the letter of each incorrect address in order on the lines below.

"   ____ ____ ____ - ____ ____ ____ ____ - ____   "

**Commas: addresses**

# Camp Correspondence

Name _____     Date _____

Add commas where needed.

Dear Sis
    Are you having fun at girls' camp? Boys' camp is great! We backpacked, hiked, and went rafting. Write back!
        See you soon
        Seth

Dear Aunt Sally
    This week at camp has been fun! Scott and I tipped over our canoe during the race.
        Your nephew
        Sal

Dear Counselor Stan
    You were the best counselor ever. Thanks for teaching me how to kayak. See you next year!
        Best regards
        Sonny

Dear Grandma
    The food is great at camp (but it's not as good as yours). I ate seventeen meatballs at dinner last night!
        Love
        Simon

Dear Mom and Dad
    Can you come pick me up from camp? A snake was found in the counselor's bed.
        Your son
        Skip

Write the words for the camp letters in the correct order.
Add commas where needed.

Thanks for sending me to camp!
        Love
        Sam

Dear Mom
Can I come back again?

How can I get my roommate to stop snoring?
Dear Dad
        Your sad son
        Steve
Please write back soon.

_____
_____
_____
        _____
        _____

_____
_____
_____
        _____
        _____

# Dino Diner

Name _____  Date _____

If commas are used correctly, cross out the letter in the "Correct" box.
If commas are needed, cross out the letter in the "Incorrect" box.
Add commas to incorrect sentences.

| Correct | Incorrect | |
|---|---|---|
| B | F | 1. Oh, I'm so glad you're serving lunch. |
| G | S | 2. To keep it healthy, I'll order a salad. |
| H | M | 3. Yes I think I would like the soup too. |
| Q | J | 4. No, I don't need a straw for my water. |
| S | L | 5. Waving wildly Dino got the waitress's attention. |
| Y | C | 6. Excuse me, but I'd like to order some french fries too. |
| D | X | 7. No I think I'll have the baked potato instead. |
| O | L | 8. After eating his soup and salad Dino tried the potato. |
| E | A | 9. After a bite, he realized the potato was cold. |
| N | I | 10. Therefore, he sent the potato back to the kitchen. |
| R | B | 11. Still Dino wasn't full and ordered pie for dessert. |
| T | R | 12. To satisfy Dino, the waitress brought him a huge piece of pie. |
| U | Z | 13. Also she refilled his water glass. |
| K | N | 14. Wow this key lime pie is tasty. |
| F | P | 15. Yes, I think I will come back again! |

## What is today's lunch special?
Match each letter that is not crossed out to a numbered line below.

" ___ ___ ___ ___ "
4   13   11   9   2   5   10   6        15   8   12   14

# Tee Time

If commas are used correctly, color the ball yellow.
Add commas to incorrect sentences.

**(A)** Tee times are set for Gomer, Gilbert, Gus, and myself.

**(M)** I bought golf shoes a hat and a glove for the tournament.

**(O)** The prizes are cash free golf lessons and new clubs.

**(X)** Bring money for fees a cart and snacks.

**(B)** I made holes in one on the 6th, 8th, and 14th holes.

**(S)** They take great care of the fairways the cart paths and the putting greens.

**(L)** Golf balls tees and towels are the pro shop's best sellers.

**(I)** I made par on holes five, nine, and ten.

**(R)** My favorite courses are in Hawaii, Georgia, and North Carolina.

**(N)** I want a hamburger french fries and a cola from the snack bar.

**(D)** I scored birdies on the 3rd, 7th, 13th, and 18th holes.

**(H)** Should I use a driver a wedge or an 8-iron for this shot?

**(I)** Gilbert won the first, second, and last holes.

**(C)** I never hit a ball in the sand lake or trees.

**(E)** Do you want to golf again on Friday, Saturday, or Sunday?

## What is a golfer's favorite animal?
To solve the riddle, write the colored letters in order on the lines below.

___     ___ ___ ___ ___ ___ ___!

©The Education Center, Inc. • *Target Reading & Writing Success* • TEC60875 • Key p. 127
**Commas: items in a series**

# Cooking for the King

Name _____   Date _____

Add commas where needed.

Monday November 8 1684

The king and queen will be served turkey mashed potatoes and apple pie.

Tuesday November 9 1684

The king will get a snack platter with nuts dates pickles and cooked apples.

Wednesday November 10 1684

Today is the queen's birthday! Her dinner will include salad bean soup and baked bananas.

Thursday November 11 1684

Prepare for the royal feast! The main course will be baked redfish shrimp lobster and beef.

Friday November 12 1684

The king the queen and their friends will have tea this afternoon.

Saturday November 13 1684

The king wants only vegetables for today's dinner. We shall serve broccoli red cabbage and carrots.

**39 Missing Commas**

Sunday November 14 1684

It's time to feed the king's sweet tooth with mints muffins tarts and hot cocoa.

Monday November 15 1684

Lady Dara will visit today! A meal will include spicy sausage custard and apple cider.

Tuesday November 16 1684

The king and queen will ask for their favorite breakfast lunch and dinner.

# Cheese, Please?

Name _____ Date _____

Add commas where needed.
Color a comma at the bottom of the page each time a comma is added.

123 Meadow Road
Mouseville WI 00001
June 14, 2004

Ms. Callie Cowley, Manager
The Cheese Factory
4200 Cheesy Avenue
Cheddar WI 00002

Dear Ms. Cowley:

I am writing to ask for your help. My friends Mark Maddie Mary and I are having a cheese-tasting contest. We are trying to see who can taste the most types of cheese in two weeks. I am in second place right now. I have tried 12 different types of cheese. My favorites are Swiss cheddar and Colby.

I was hoping you could send me some samples of your cheese. I would like to try Gouda Muenster Edam and blue. Should I pay you with cash a check or a money order?

Sincerely

Mike Mouse

_Me eating cheese._

| , | , | , | , | , | , |
|---|---|---|---|---|---|

| , | , | , | , | , | , | , |
|---|---|---|---|---|---|---|

# A "Bee-utiful" Hive

Name _____     Date _____

If commas are used correctly, color the shape to show the path to the queen.
Cross out commas that are not
    used correctly.
Add commas where needed.

1. Amazingly, tens of thousands of honeybees live in one colony.

2. The queen, the drones, and the workers can all be found inside the hive.

3. The bees use the honeycomb to raise their young, and to keep food.

4. Yes the worker bees build the honeycomb with wax.

5. Guard bees will attack bears humans, and bees from outside the colony.

6. The honeybee has a head, a thorax, and an abdomen.

7. In addition a bee has five eyes.

8. However bees cannot focus their eyes, or see the color red.

9. A worker bee's legs are used to walk, to clean its body, and to handle wax.

10. Did you know that a bee can fly forward sideways and backward?

11. Also a bee can hover in place in the air.

12. A bee can distinguish blue, yellow and ultraviolet rays.

13. Muscles inside the bee's mouth suck nectar up its tongue, through its mouth, and into its stomach.

14. Unfortunately, a bee sting causes pain and produces swelling.

**Commas: introductory words and phrases, items in a series**

# Paint by Number

Name _____ Date _____

If commas are used correctly, color the paint splotch red.
If commas are needed, color the paint splotch blue.

1. Everyone be sure to read the instructions.

2. Pete, please pass me the jar of yellow paint.

3. Watch out for that wet paint Paco.

4. Perry, will you show me how to create a shadow?

5. Penny, don't forget to soak your brushes overnight.

6. Sketch your drawing in pencil first Pam.

7. Paul, we need more purple paint.

8. Polly you'll need to let the paint dry first.

9. That is a lovely painting, Perry.

10. Pat look at the painting I just finished.

Rewrite each incorrect sentence, adding commas where needed.

_____

_____

_____

_____

_____

# A "Fin-Tastic" School

Name _____ Date _____

Underline the appositive in each sentence.
Add commas where needed.

Hint: An **appositive** is a word or phrase that renames or further explains the noun it follows.

1. Our teacher Mrs. Finley loves to teach grammar.

2. Mackie Reel the smartest kid in school won the spelling bee.

3. He spelled *hippopotamus* the hardest word in his category.

4. Today I have smoked sardines my favorite lunch.

5. Barry Cuda my best friend sits next to me in math class.

6. We are making small floats and masks for Mardi Gras a festival.

7. We learned about oceanography a part of geography that includes oceans, seas, and marine life.

8. Our school football team the Fighting Fins won the game.

9. I tried out for the lead role in *Five Fishy Friends* the school play.

10. My class is going on a field trip to Aquatic World the new aquarium.

11. My science fair project Exploring the World's Oceans won first prize.

12. Today we read *Three Fish in the Ocean* my favorite book.

13. Bea Fish a children's author is visiting our school next week.

14. I have homework in math and reading my two favorite subjects.

15. Tomorrow is Friday the best day of the week!

# Meet the Daisy Family

Name _____ Date _____

If commas are used correctly, color the flower yellow.
Add commas where needed.
Cross out a comma on the wall each time you add one.

1. The Daisy family originally from Texas loves sunshine.

2. They grow at the Daisy Dot, a small garden.

3. Dalton, what was yesterday's temperature?

4. It was 78 degrees yesterday Dena.

5. Dan, will you pass the watering can?

6. Dana the tallest flower grew two inches in three days.

7. Did you see that dragonfly Damon?

8. Drew, the oldest, likes to sway in the wind.

9. Delia the youngest flower likes to play in the rain.

10. Donny that's the most colorful butterfly I've ever seen!

11. The Daisys' friends the Roses live next door.

12. Dena, will you bring some water for the Roses?

Commas: appositives, direct address

# Travel Troubles

If quotation marks are used correctly, color the lily pad in the yes column.
If quotation marks are used incorrectly, color the lily pad in the no column.

|   |   | yes | no |
|---|---|-----|----|
| 1. | How far have we traveled? "asked Fran." | X | O |
| 2. | "We've gone about 130 miles," answered Fred. | D | R |
| 3. | "The car is sounding a bit strange," replied Fran. | T | P |
| 4. | Don't "worry, said" Fred. | S | I |
| 5. | "The car just stopped! exclaimed" Fran. | Q | Z |
| 6. | "Let me see," said Fred, "if I can fix this." | F | B |
| 7. | "What do you think it is? asked Fran. | C | A |
| 8. | "Watch out! yelled Fran. The radiator is steaming!" | V | K |
| 9. | "Thanks for the warning," answered Fred. | E | M |
| 10. | "Then Fran shouted, "Be careful! Don't stand too close to the road. | N | H |
| 11. | "I know," answered Fred. "Those cars are zooming by." | G | W |
| 12. | With a sigh, Fred said, "I don't think I can fix this." | L | J |

## What did Fred do with the car?

To find out, match the colored letters to the numbered lines below.

__ __   __ __ __   __ __   __ __ __ " __ __ __ __ "
10 9    10 7 2    4 3     3  1  7  2

__ __ __ !
1  6  6

# Trail Talk

Add quotation marks where needed.

1. Sighing, Bob said, It's been a long day on the trail.

2. I feel like I've been eating dust all day, grumbled Arnie.

3. You should've worn a bandana like me, said Lou with a grin.

4. Arnie rubbed his belly and said, I think I'll cook some chili.

5. I need a few more logs for the campfire, called Arnie.

6. Bob and Lou moaned and said, Oh, we'll go and get some.

7. Keep an eye out for coyotes! exclaimed Arnie. I heard one howl.

8. Is supper ready yet? I'm hungry! whined Lou.

9. I smell something good! yelled Bob.

10. Is it our supper? asked Lou.

11. It is, answered Arnie. Let's eat!

12. Bob laughed and said, I'd rather eat chili than dust any day!

Complete a sentence for each character on the lines below. Punctuate correctly.

13. Bob shouted, _____

_____

14. Arnie said, _____

_____

15. Lou whispered, _____

_____

# Game Day

If quotation marks are used correctly, color the baseball.
Add quotation marks where needed.
The number of colored baseballs should equal the
Lions' score.

**TIGERS    10**
**LIONS      5**

1) Al the announcer roared, It's a grand day for Tiger baseball!"

2) It's a warm, sunny day, he said.

3) Fanny asked, "What time does the game start?"

4) The crowd cheered, Go Tigers! Go Tigers!

5) "Hot dogs! Sodas! Cotton candy! yelled Vinny the vendor.

6) Coach Growly told his team, We need to play hard today!

7) The umpire called, "Batter up!"

8) Hit a homer, Tim! yelled Fanny.

9) "I'll take three hot dogs with extra chili," Fred told Vinny.

10) The umpire shouted, "Foul ball!"

11) Heads up, fans. Here comes a fly ball!" Al shouted.

12) Vinny shouted, That almost hit me!

13) Did you see that ball sail out of the park? Fanny asked.

14) "Get up for the seventh-inning stretch," Al announced.

15) The game's over, Al howled. The Tigers win!

# Quick Fix?

Name _____  Date _____

Match each direct quote with an indirect quote.
Write the matching letter in the bolt.

The radio blared, "Get tip-top service at Fletcher's Garage!"

Fletcher asked, "What's wrong with your truck, Mr. Yota?"

"The horn doesn't work," Troy Yota told Fletcher.

"I can't get my car into first gear!" blurted Sue Barroo.

Fletcher said, "I need to test-drive your car, Sue."

Cora Vet cut in and said, "My car's brake pedal squeaks."

"Would you check the fuel filter too?" Cora asked.

Fletcher told Cora, "Your car needs a tune-up."

**A.** Troy Yota said that the horn in his truck does not work.

**B.** Fletcher told Cora that her car needs a tune-up.

**C.** The radio ad said that the service at Fletcher's Garage is tip-top.

**D.** Cora asked Fletcher to check her car's fuel filter.

**E.** Sue Barroo said that her car won't go into first gear.

**F.** Cora Vet said that her car's brake pedal squeaks.

**G.** Fletcher asked Mr. Yota what was wrong with his truck.

**H.** Fletcher said that he needs to test-drive Sue's car.

# Jump!

Name _____ Date _____

If the sentence is an indirect quote, color the letter in the
   indirect column.

If the sentence has a direct quote, color the letter in the
   direct column. Then add quotation marks where needed.

| Direct | Indirect | |
|---|---|---|
| O | U | 1. Coach Kay said, Let's practice making jump shots. |
| E | N | 2. Coach Kay said that we need to work on our layups. |
| P | S | 3. Get the ball and face the basket! Coach Kay shouted. |
| G | I | 4. Coach Kirby will help us out this week, said Coach Kay. |
| O | M | 5. Coach Kirby said that he'll teach us how to dunk! |
| J | B | 6. Split up into two groups, Coach Kay said. |
| C | F | 7. Coach Kirby said that he'd take the first group. |
| W | R | 8. Coach Kay said, I'm going to teach you to jump-stop. |
| K | T | 9. Jump, said Coach Kay. Then catch the ball and land. |
| A | G | 10. Coach Kirby said that Coach Kay used to be his coach. |
| Q | L | 11. He said, I'll teach you how to dribble behind your backs. |
| P | H | 12. Right now, Coach Kirby stated, let's work on jump balls. |
| D | J | 13. Coach Kirby said that it takes timing to get a jump ball. |
| V | Y | 14. Okay, let's switch groups! yelled Coach Kay. |
| G | X | 15. Coach Kirby said, Now I'll teach you how to dunk! |

## Why are basketball players messy eaters?

To solve the riddle, match the uncolored letters to the numbered lines below.

___ ___ ___ ___ ___ ___ ___    ___ ___ ___ ___    ___ ___ ___ ___ ___ ___ ___ !
 6   2   7  10   1   3   2      9  12   2  14     13   8   4   6   6  11   2

# We All Scream for Ice Cream!

Name _____ Date _____

If the punctuation is correct, color the matching ice-cream scoop brown.
If the punctuation is incorrect, color the matching ice-cream scoop yellow.

1. Ira asked, "What's that sound I hear?"

2. "It's Ike's ice-cream truck!" squealed Ida with delight.

3. "Hurry up" Ivan said "and don't forget to bring your money."

4. "What'll you have?", Ike asked.

5. "I'd like a rocky road ice-cream cone with two scoops" Ira replied.

6. Ida asked, "Do you have frozen lemonade today?"

7. "I'll have a chocolate chip ice-cream sandwich" Ira chimed in.

8. "This is so cold it makes my eyeballs hurt!" Ida exclaimed.

9. "Do you have rainbow ice pops," Ivan asked?

10. Ike answered, "No, but I've got orange dream bars!"

11. Ike started up the truck and said, "It's time to be going. See you tomorrow!"

12. "We'll be waiting," everyone yelled!

Write the number of an incorrect sentence in each scoop.
Then rewrite each sentence correctly.

**Quotations marks: commas in direct quotes**

# Off 'n' Running

Name _____ Date _____

Add commas and quotation marks where needed.

**Start**

1. Tina asked Hey, Tammy, are you ready to run?

2. It's so early Tammy groaned.

3. Why don't we warm up a little first? Tammy asked.

4. Tina suggested Let's walk for a couple of minutes to warm up.

5. Tammy said Okay. I think I'm ready.

6. There's a 5K race next month Tina commented.

7. A 5K race! Tammy exclaimed. How many miles are in a 5K race?

8. It's only 3.1 miles Tina explained.

9. We run two miles every day Tina continued.

10. Two long miles Tammy grumbled.

11. Come on Tina begged. It will be fun!

12. Tina chanted We're going to run in a 5K race.

13. Shhh, I'm training muttered Tammy.

14. I'm training to run my first 5K race Tammy said with a smile.

**Finish**

# Lots of Loot

Name _____     Date _____

Circle each letter that should be capitalized.
Color the jewel with the matching letter.

Letters on jewels: G, T, W, T, L, I, W, C, T, I, W, T, A, A, L, L, T, I, N

1. Captain Claw said, "the sky looks dark and gloomy."

2. "we'll never make it to the island," Feathers groaned.

3. Feathers whined, "the ship's rocking is making me sick."

4. The crew begged, "captain, can we please turn back?"

5. "no!" bellowed the captain. "we will find the treasure."

6. "look!" squawked Redbeard. "there is land ahead!"

7. Blue Beak climbed the mast and declared, "ahoy! He's right!"

8. "it will be our pleasure," Feathers sang, "to find the hidden treasure."

9. "the waves are dying down," Captain Claw noted.

10. The captain ordered, "get close to the sandy beach."

11. "aye, aye, Captain," Blue Beak whistled with a salute.

12. Feathers called, "last one off the ship is a rotten bird!"

13. "look there," Blue Beak called. "is that the treasure chest?"

14. "it is!" Redbeard shouted. "we're rich!"

Quotation marks: capitalization in direct quotes

# Down on the Farm

If quotations marks and punctuation are used correctly, circle the sentence number.

1. Morgan trotted in and asked, "What's for breakfast?"

2. "you want breakfast already," April asked?

3. "The rooster just barely crowed," she added.

4. "okay." whinnied Morgan, "I'll just have oats again,"

5. pa wants us to move some hay. April told Morgan.

6. "We'll have to take the tractor," she added.

7. "Whose turn is it to drive?" Morgan asked.

8. aw, it's your turn, April said. "I drove last week".

9. Well, are you ready to go? asked" Morgan.

10. "No, fussed April" I still have to eat!

Write the number of an incorrect sentence in each bowl.
Then rewrite each sentence correctly.

_____
_____
_____
_____
_____
_____

# Curl Up and Read

Name _____  Date _____

If the sentence is correct, color the curler with the matching number green.
If the sentence is incorrect, color the curler with the matching number red.
Then add quotation marks where needed.

1. Paul handed Pat last week's issue of <u>Quill Quotes</u>.

2. Pat flipped to an article called "Sharp Talk."

3. Pat read a poem called Ode to a Comb out loud.

4. Paul said it made him think about Pretty Prickly, his favorite song.

5. Paul told Pat that one of the book's chapters was titled "The Comb Out."

6. Pat picked up a magazine called <u>Quills for Kids</u>.

7. The Hokey-Pokey, the song Pat liked best, came on the radio.

8. Paul said he loved the song Comb, Comb, Comb Your Quill.

9. Pat asked if Paul had seen the movie called <u>The Pink Porcupine</u>.

10. Paul said he loved its theme song, Think Pink.

11. Pat asked if the song came from the poem When I Think of You.

12. Pat turned to Quick Quill Curls and read the article to Paul.

13. Paul told Pat that she should read the article "I Am Not a Hedgehog."

14. Paul said This Is Me is the title of the book's first chapter.

Hint: Use **quotation marks** around the titles of poems, articles, songs, and book chapters. **Underline** book, magazine, and movie titles.

# The Perfect Match

Name _____ Date _____

Match the pictures to find out which item belongs to each person.
Add **'s** to show ownership.
The first one has been done for you.

| | | | |
|---|---|---|---|
| shopper | | sneakers | |
| owner | | loafers | |
| buyer | | flats | |
| person | | shoes | |
| mother | | shoe polish | |
| clerk | | sandals | |
| ballerina | | boots | |
| salesperson | | clogs | |
| child | | flip-flops | |
| sister | | socks | |
| brother | | cleats | |
| father | | slippers | |

_ballerina's_
_slippers_ _____

_____     _____     _____

_____     _____     _____

_____     _____     _____

_____     _____     _____

# Down by the Sea

Name _____ Date _____

If apostrophes are used correctly, circle the sentence number.
Cross out apostrophes that are not used correctly, and then add apostrophes where needed.
Color an apostrophe on a float each time you add one.

1. This years' vacation for the Penguin family was at the beach.

2. Their parents' cottage is right by the ocean.

3. Pete and his brothers saw many animal's homes on the beach.

4. The first things they found were two hermit crabs' shells.

5. Then they noticed some sea turtles nests.

6. His two sisters' towels were lying next to several sea stars.

7. The sea stars skin looked bumpy and rough.

8. Then his little brothers' ball rolled behind some dunes.

9. The dunes tall grasses made it hard to see the ball.

10. The boys found the ball, and then they saw dolphins fins in the water.

11. The dolphins' were playing with a friends Frisbee disks.

12. Pete and his brothers and sisters joined the dolphins' game.

13. Then they invited the dolphins to their parents' house for dinner.

14. The next day, the Penguin family went sailing in two neighbor's boats.

15. Everyone agreed this was the Penguins' best trip ever!

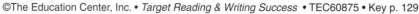

# Shop 'til You Drop

Name _____  Date _____

Write the word in the blank that best completes each sentence.
If the word you wrote is a possessive noun, color the tag at the beginning of the sentence.

**M** Look at all these _____! (clothes, clothes')

**T** My favorite _____ are red and orange. (outfits, outfits')

**S** Those _____ shoes are neat. (girls, girls')

**L** I'll put those _____ back on their hangers. (sweaters, sweaters')

**N** Both _____ colors are too dull. (shirts, shirts')

**V** Look! These _____ are on sale! (belts, belts')

**O** I would love to have two _____ of pants. (pairs, pairs')

**A** All the _____ legs are too long for me. (pants, pants')

**I** Let's each try on one of those _____! (dresses, dresses')

**K** The _____ styles look great on you! (dresses, dresses')

**E** Both _____ sizes are too small. (shirts, shirts')

**R** The _____ bows match the dresses perfectly. (hats, hats')

**W** What _____ are you going to buy? (items, items')

**G** I think I'll get two _____ and a dress. (hats, hats')

**S** The _____ total cost is $43.36. (items, items')

## What do some reptiles wear on their feet?

To solve the riddle, write the letters from the colored tags in order on the lines below.

" ____ ____  ____ ____ ____ ____ "

©The Education Center, Inc. • *Target Reading & Writing Success* • TEC60875 • Key p. 129

**Apostrophes: plural and possessive nouns**

# Horsin' Around

Name _____    Date _____

Rewrite each phrase and use an apostrophe to show possession.
The first one has been done for you.

1. reins of two horses
   _horses' reins_____

2. brush of one groomer
   _____ (R)

3. stables of five horses
   _____ (L)

4. saddles of three owners
   _____ (I)

5. food of one horse
   _____ (A)

6. stalls of four horses
   _____ (T)

7. bridles of one horse
   _____ (N)

8. trails of two ranches
   _____ (L)

9. hooves of six horses
   _____ (E)

10. manes of eight horses
    _____ (C)

11. horseshoes of one horse
    _____ (M)

12. blankets of three riders
    _____ (O)

13. hay of one dozen horses
    _____ (L)

14. trophy of one rider
    _____ (U)

15. corral of ten horses
    _____ (T)

**Why did the horse put on a blanket?**

To solve the riddle, write the letter of each plural possessive
phrase in order on the lines below.

He was a ___ ___ _T_ ___ ___ ___

" ___ ___ ___ ___ "!

**Apostrophes: singular and plural possessive nouns**

# Strike!

Name _____ Date _____

If apostrophes are used correctly, color the bowling ball.
Cross out apostrophes that are not used correctly, and then add apostrophes where needed.
Color a bowling pin each time you add an apostrophe.

1. Both teams best bowler's are going first.

2. The player's shirts are green.

3. Steve's team has blue bowling balls.

4. Where are the first bowlers' shoes?

5. The shoes are in each player's bag.

6. The first two bowler's scores were 234 and 268.

7. The Super Strikers average score is 273.

8. Their star player's score is 296.

9. Now it is the Bayside Bowlers turn.

10. Knock M. Down's first ball went into the gutter.

11. The players second ball was a strike!

12. Now the teams scores are almost even.

13. It is Steve Strike's turn to bowl.

14. This players' scores are always the highest.

15. Steves team has won the championship!

# At the Hive

Use the numbers on each bee's wings to find a word pair on the hive.
Rewrite each word pair to make a contraction.
The first one has been done for you.

1
3

_____ I've _____

20
15

13
19

12
4

9
11

_____     _____     _____     _____

14
15

16
18

10
7

5
3

_____          _____     _____

17
11

10
6

| | 1. | | |
| | I | | |
| 2. | | 3. | |
| am | | have | |
| 4. | 5. | | 6. |
| had | should | | are |
| | 7. | 8. | |
| | will | has | |
| 9. | 10. | | 11. |
| was | they | | not |
| | 12. | 13. | |
| | she | we | |
| 14. | 15. | | 16. |
| he | is | | you |
| | 17. | 18. | |
| | do | would | |
| 19. | 20. | | |
| were | it | | |

1
2

_____

8
11

_____

**Apostrophes: contractions**

# An "Eggs-citing" Time

Name _____  Date _____

Rewrite each word pair to make a contraction.
Circle the letter(s) that the apostrophe replaced.
The first one has been done for you.

1. here (is)

here's

2. she will

3. he is

4. you are

5. they will

6. would not

7. who is

8. should have

9. she is

10. were not

Write the two words that form each contraction on the eggshell.

11. what's

12. she'd

13. wasn't

14. there's

15. there'll

16. we've

17. haven't

18. he'll

Apostrophes: contractions

45

# Is It Time?

Name _____ Date _____

Rewrite the time on each appointment card using a colon.
The first one has been done for you.

1. **Dan Chers**
Monday
two thirty-five
**2:35**
(I)

2. **S. Miles**
Monday
seven fifty-eight
_____
(A)

3. **B. R. Aces**
Monday
eight thirty
_____
(T)

4. **Phil A. Tooth**
Monday
twelve fifteen
_____
(F)

5. **Anita Crown**
Tuesday
eleven forty-five
_____
(O)

6. **E. Namel**
Tuesday
two fifty
_____
(T)

7. **Floss Yurteeth**
Wednesday
four twenty
_____
(H)

8. **Nomar Cavity**
Wednesday
ten forty
_____
(R)

9. **Mo Larr**
Thursday
three ten
_____
(Y)

10. **B. I. Cuspid**
Thursday
six fifty-five
_____
(O)

11. **Eva Brushin**
Friday
three twenty-five
_____
(T)

12. **Phil Ling**
Friday
one forty-five
_____
(T)

13. **Willy Grin**
Friday
ten thirty
_____
(R)

14. **Pearl E. White**
Monday
four twenty-five
_____
(E)

15. **N. O. Sugar**
Wednesday
ten twenty
_____
(!)

## What's the best time to visit the dentist?
To solve the riddle, match the circled letters to the numbered lines below.

"  ___ ___ ___ ___ ___   - I ___ ___ ___ ___ ___  "

| 7:58 | 12:15 | 2:50 | 4:25 | 10:40 | | 8:30 | 6:55 | 11:45 | 1:45 | 4:20 | | 2:35 | 10:30 | 3:25 | 3:10 | 10:20 |

**Colon: hours, minutes**

# Plannin' a Picnic

Name _____     Date _____

Add colons where they are needed.

1. These days might be good for a beach picnic Friday, Sunday, or Monday.

2. We could invite four friends Olive, Otis, Opal, and Oscar.

3. The last time, we had too much junk food chips, cookies, and candy.

4. This time, let's bring healthier snacks like these fruit, nuts, or cheese.

5. We can grill the following burgers, hot dogs, and corn.

6. Let's bring these drinks water, fruit juice, and soda.

7. We'll need these paper products plates, napkins, and cups.

Unscramble the sentence on each ball. Write it on the lines below. Add colons where needed.

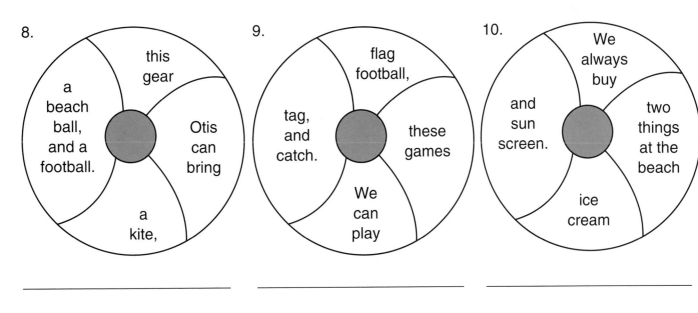

8.

this gear

a beach ball, and a football.

Otis can bring

a kite,

9.

flag football,

tag, and catch.

these games

We can play

10.

We always buy

and sun screen.

two things at the beach

ice cream

_____

_____

_____

_____

# Rhino Reports

Name _____     Date _____

Add colons where they are needed.
Color a tack each time a colon is added.

## Dr. Ryan O. Ceros

### Winner of the Hornel Prize in Rhino Studies

Dr. Ceros will speak about two types of rhinos the black rhino and the white rhino.

Monday at 7 00 P.M.

Dr. Ceros will talk about what rhinos eat grass, leafy twigs, and shrubs.

Tuesday at 10 00 A.M.

Learn about these rhino traits horns, thick skin, and three-toed feet.

Monday at 11 00 A.M.

Watch a film about where wild rhinos roam Africa and Asia.

Monday at 6 00 P.M.
Thursday at 10 00 A.M.

Dr. Ceros will sign copies of his latest books *The Rhino's Plant-Eating Pals* and *The Rhino's Meat-Eating Neighbors*.

Saturday from 2 30 P.M. until 4 00 P.M.

Sign up at any of these shops Student Central, Book Inn, or Readers Corner.

Colons: review

# Feather Fluff

Name _____ Date _____

If extra information is given in parentheses, color the box in that column.

If an abbreviated name of a company or an organization is in parentheses, color the box in that column.

| | more information | abbreviation |
|---|:---:|:---:|
| 1. This is Felix's first day of work as a (feather) fluffer. | E | O |
| 2. Felix got the job after an Order of the Feather Fluffer (OFF) meeting. | T | S |
| 3. The chief fluffer from Idaho's Fine Feathers (IFF) was there. | I | T |
| 4. The IFF chief (Fran Prince) gave Felix her card. | O | N |
| 5. So Felix called her toll-free number (1-555-463-5833). | N | E |
| 6. Felix told Fran that he went to Feather State College (FSC). | U | C |
| 7. Fran also went to FSC (four years earlier). | L | H |
| 8. Fran and Felix both took the same class (How to Fluff Fine Feathers). | E | T |
| 9. Felix was a member of the Fowl Against Flat Feathers Group (FAFFG). | O | B |
| 10. Felix won first prize for fluffing at the First Annual Bird Bash (FABB). | D | G |
| 11. Fran (who was impressed) offered Felix the job. | F | E |
| 12. Felix (who had always wanted to work there) accepted the job. | H | S |

## On which side do peacocks have more feathers?

To find out, write the letter that is not colored for each number below.

___ ___    ___ ___ ___    ___ ___ ___ ___ ___ ___ ___
1   4      2   7   5      9   6   8   12  3   10  11

**Parentheses** **49**

# Pencil Me In

Name _____    Date _____

Add parentheses where they are needed.
The first one has been done for you.

What did one pencil say to the other?

1.  I have to be at school early (by 7:15) Friday.
    S          C     M     Y

2.  I'm going to the Student Writing Crew SWC meeting.
    A      P           Y  O

3.  I'll be writing the meeting's minutes report of what happened.
    O     N     U         L

4.  The last meeting two weeks ago lasted for one hour.
    O     O     E     A

5.  This week's meeting should be half as long 30 minutes.
    S   H        K     S

6.  Ms. Penny the SWC sponsor said there are two new writing contests.
    H     A         C    T

7.  I am going to enter the Have Pencil Will Travel HPWT writing contest.
    A     P   R   P

8.  The Putting It on Paper Company PIPC is having a contest too.
    O   M     T   O

9.  If you want to enter, call their toll-free number 1-555-667-2797.
    B     U    N     I

10. The Write and Refine Group WRG helps sponsor the SWC.
    F  I     G  H

To solve the riddle above, write the letter under each
parenthesis in order on the lines below.

" ____ ____ , ____ ____ ____   ____ ____ ____ ____

____ ____ ____ ____ ____   ____ ____ ____ ____ ____ T !"

Grammar and Usage

# Grammar and Usage
## Table of Contents

# Parent Communication and Student Checkups
*See pages 112–123 for corresponding parent communication and student checkups (mini tests) for these skills.

# Nothin' but Net

Name _____    Date _____

Decide whether the underlined nouns are common or proper.
Write each noun on the matching basketball goal.

1. <u>Sheila</u> Shooter plays professional <u>basketball</u>.

2. The <u>name</u> of her team is the <u>Dribblers</u>.

3. <u>Robin</u> is Sheila's best <u>friend</u> on the team.

4. <u>Fans</u> always cheer for them to shoot <u>baskets</u>.

5. The Dribblers play their <u>games</u> in <u>Raleigh</u> and Durham.

6. <u>Coach Net</u> asks her <u>players</u> to try hard every game.

7. *Athletes Today* featured Robin in a magazine <u>article</u>.

8. <u>Referees</u> from <u>Charlotte</u> officiate all the home games.

9. <u>Star Arena</u> is the location of the away game on <u>Monday</u>.

## Common Nouns

_____    _____

_____    _____

_____    _____

## Proper Nouns

_____    _____

_____    _____

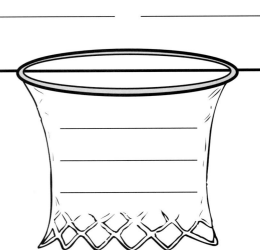

_____

_____

_____

# Fun in the Sun

Name _____     Date _____

If the noun is singular, write its plural form.
If the noun is plural, write its singular form.

1. shell
_____

2. beach
_____

3. children
_____

4. fish
_____

5. glasses
_____

6. waves
_____

7. shovel
_____

8. men
_____

9. feet
_____

10. soda
_____

11. leaf
_____

12. lunches
_____

13. box
_____

14. tooth
_____

15. radio
_____

16. fly
_____

**Nouns: singular, plural**

# Possessive Pups

Name _____  Date _____

If the possessive noun is singular, color the tag red.
If the possessive noun is plural, color the tag blue.

1. Danny's dogs
S

2. dogs' collars
B

3. pup's house
R

4. dogs' chew toys
L

5. Max's leashes
R

6. dogs' new tricks
O

7. puppy's obedience school
W

8. puppies' owner
N

9. dog's treats
I

10. children's pet
D

11. pup's water bowl
O

12. dogs' toys
I

13. animal's vet
N

14. puppies' food
E

## Which dog does the bone belong to?

To answer the question, write the letters from the blue-colored tags in order on the lines below.

____  ____  ____  ____  ____  ____  ____

# Bubble Action!

Name _____  Date _____

Color the bubbles that have action verbs.

am

think

breathe

would

is

must

dreamed

did

sunk

listen

hear

drifted

can

caught

climbed

throw

rise

floated

wrote

wondered

BUBBLE MACHINE

Write three more action verbs in the bubbles below. Write a sentence using each verb.

_____

_____

_____

**Verbs: action**

# Really Big Fish Story

Name _____ Date _____

Circle each helping verb.
Box its main verb.

1. Mike, Meredith, and I were fishing one day.

2. We hoped each of us would catch a fish.

3. I wondered if I could sit on the boat long enough.

4. Suddenly, something was pulling on Meredith's line!

5. We thought we would see a huge fish!

6. The weight of the fish was bending the fishing pole.

7. Meredith was grasping the fishing pole tightly.

8. We told her she should reel it in quickly.

9. Remember that a large fish can pull you off a boat.

10. All three of us were trying to pull in the fish.

11. Suddenly, we were looking at Meredith's giant fish.

12. Instead of a fish, Meredith had caught a whale!

13. Who would believe us?

14. Three minnows had caught a huge whale!

15. You should tell this story to your friends!

# Let's Dance, Partner!

Name _____ Date _____

Underline the linking verb in each sentence.
Write each linking verb in the matching chain link.

1. Luke's new friend looks friendly to me.
2. Her perfume smells nice, doesn't it?
3. Luke grew restless waiting for his friend to arrive.
4. That band sounds lively tonight!
5. The party hostess seemed happy with the number of guests.
6. Lisa remained calm until her partner arrived.
7. Liz became upset when the band stopped playing.
8. Liz and Lisa were sorry they couldn't dance all night.

1.    2.    3.    4.    5.    6.    8.    7.

Use a linking verb from the chain above to complete each sentence below.
Then draw an arrow to connect the two words that the verb links.
The first one has been done for you.

9. The crowd ( grew ) very excited as the band played.

10. Larry and Luke ( ) happy to be invited.

11. This new music ( ) perfect for dancing.

12. Liz ( ) fantastic in her new dance outfit.

13. Lisa ( ) a dancer when she was four years old.

14. Lisa ( ) sad when the dance was over.

15. Lulu ( ) friends with her dance partner.

**Verbs: linking**

# Walking a Proverbial Path

Name _____  Date _____

Complete each proverb using a present tense verb from the word bank.
Write its matching letter in the box.

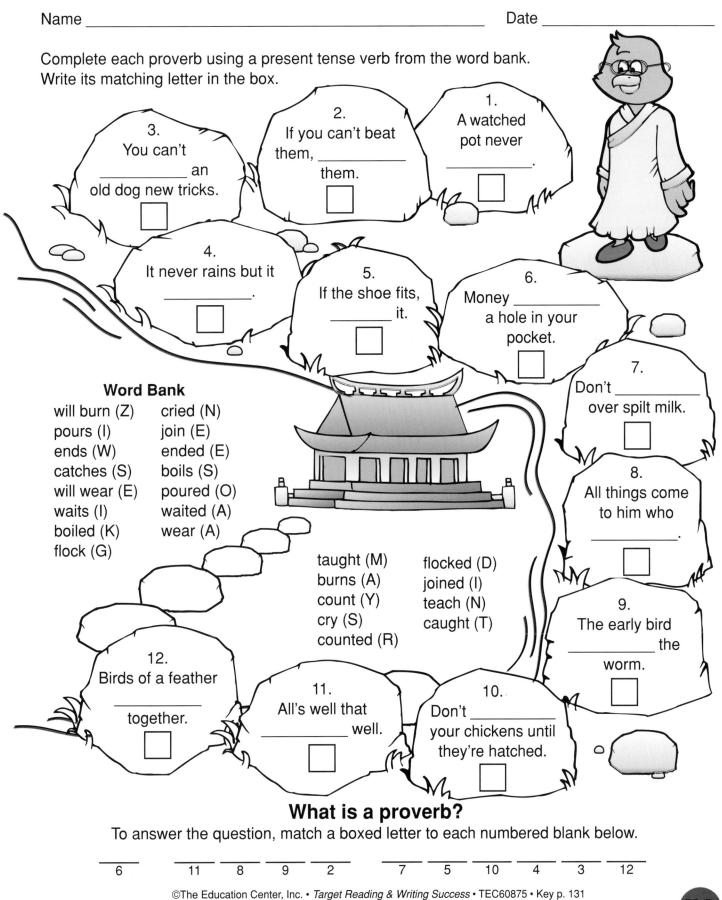

**3.**
You can't
_____ an
old dog new tricks.
☐

**2.**
If you can't beat
them, _____
them.
☐

**1.**
A watched
pot never
_____ .
☐

**4.**
It never rains but it
_____ .
☐

**5.**
If the shoe fits,
_____ it.
☐

**6.**
Money _____
a hole in your
pocket.
☐

**7.**
Don't _____
over spilt milk.
☐

**8.**
All things come
to him who
_____ .
☐

**9.**
The early bird
_____ the
worm.
☐

### Word Bank
will burn (Z)      cried (N)
pours (I)          join (E)
ends (W)           ended (E)
catches (S)        boils (S)
will wear (E)      poured (O)
waits (I)          waited (A)
boiled (K)         wear (A)
flock (G)

taught (M)     flocked (D)
burns (A)      joined (I)
count (Y)      teach (N)
cry (S)        caught (T)
counted (R)

**12.**
Birds of a feather
_____
together.
☐

**11.**
All's well that
_____ well.
☐

**10.**
Don't _____
your chickens until
they're hatched.
☐

## What is a proverb?
To answer the question, match a boxed letter to each numbered blank below.

___  ___  ___  ___  ___  ___  ___  ___  ___  ___  ___
6    11   8    9    2         7    5    10   4    3    12

©The Education Center, Inc. • *Target Reading & Writing Success* • TEC60875 • Key p. 131

**Verbs: present tense**

**59**

# A Puzzling Past Event

Name _____   Date _____

Complete each sentence using the past tense of the verb in parentheses.

What does this mean?

Croatoan

1.

What _____ to the Lost Colony, England's second colony in America? (happen)

2.

In 1587, Sir Walter Raleigh _____ a group to settle at Chesapeake Bay. (want)

3.

But the ships' commander _____ to sail past Roanoke Island. (refuse)

4.

John White, the colony's leader, and the 117 colonists were _____ to land there. (force)

5.

John White's granddaughter was born in August, 27 days after the settlers _____. (arrive)

6.

She was the first English child born in America. They _____ her Virginia Dare. (name)

7.

Later in August, White _____ back to England for supplies. (travel)

8.

He _____ back to the colony three years later. (sail)

9.

A war between England and Spain _____ him from returning sooner. (prevent)

10.

When White finally arrived, he _____ that no one lived there anymore. (learn)

11.

He found the letters C, R, and O _____ on one tree and the word Croatoan carved on another. (carve)

12.

Because of a storm, White _____ his search for the colonists. (stop)

13.

He _____ to England without finding the colonists. (return)

14.

Some historians believe that the colonists _____ in battles with unfriendly Indians. (die)

15.

Other people think that the colonists _____ several different Indian tribes. (join)

# Fast-Forward to the Future!

Name _____ Date _____

Rewrite each sentence using the future tense.
The first one has been done for you.

1. Freda Fly visited her family on Friday.

   _Freda Fly will visit her family on Friday._

2. Her cousin Fred greets her first.

   _____

3. Then the other family members swarm around her.

   _____

4. Grandma Fly squeezes lemons for lemonade.

   _____

5. Freda sipped her favorite drink.

   _____

6. Her brother buzzed around her in circles.

   _____

7. Freda stays with her family until 5:00 P.M.

   _____

8. Her aunt prepared a picnic to celebrate Freda's visit.

   _____

9. Freda tasted everything!

   _____

10. Then she waved goodbye.

    _____

# "A-maze-ing" Voyage

Name _____   Date _____

If the present and past tense of each verb pair are correct, circle the pair.
Connect the circled pairs to show the submarine's path through the cave.

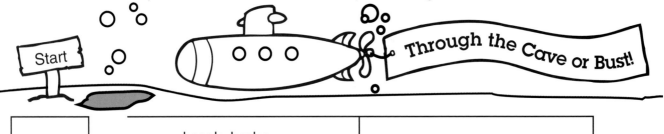

Start

Through the Cave or Bust!

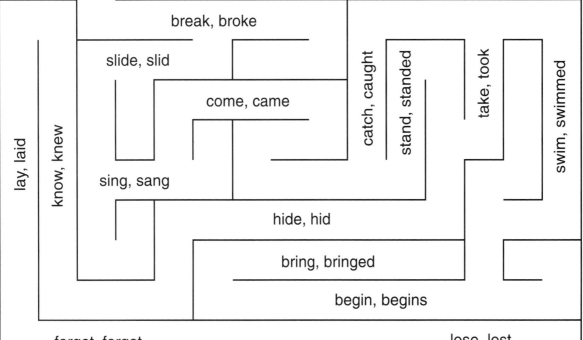

break, broke

slide, slid

come, came

catch, caught

stand, standed

take, took

swim, swimmed

lay, laid

know, knew

sing, sang

hide, hid

bring, bringed

begin, begins

forget, forgot

lose, lost

pay, payed

give, gove

leave, leaved

spin, spinned

go, goed

keep, keeped

run, runned

drive, drived

sit, sat

say, sayed

Finish

# It's a Hoedown!

Name _____  Date _____

Rewrite each sentence using the correct past tense or past participle form of the verb.

1. Bessie hang a sign about Friday night's hoedown.

   _____

   _____

2. She had grow nervous about the details.

   _____

   _____

3. Then she throw herself into getting things done.

   _____

   _____

4. She had meets with the banjo and bass fiddle players.

   _____

5. At 1:00 P.M., her cousin Butch brings bales of hay for the guests to sit on.

   _____

6. Bessie had sets out the punch bowl and cups at 3:00 P.M.

   _____

7. At 4:00 P.M., her sister begin to hang crepe paper.

   _____

8. By 5:00 P.M., Bessie had leaves to get dressed.

   _____

9. She gets back to the barn at 6 P.M.

   _____

10. She had goes over the plans with Tony Pony, the square dance caller.

    _____

11. At 7:00 P.M., the band breaks into music.

    _____

12. The guests slide onto the floor.

    _____

# A Tense Time

Name _____ Date _____

Underline the verb or verb phrase in each sentence.
Color by the code.

**Porphon**

1.
An unmanned spaceship is on its way to the planet Porphon.

2.
This ship carries a new probe in its cargo bay.

3.
With luck the probe will land on the planet without any damage.

4.
The probe will study the planet's soil for four days.

5.
It will rove over the planet's surface at three miles per hour.

6.
Its camera has enough film for thousands of pictures.

**Color Code**
present tense = red
past tense = yellow
future tense = black

7.
A satellite will transmit the pictures to Earth.

8.
Will the probe find proof of life?

9.
On the ship's last mission, a probe gathered a rock.

10.
The rock contained a substance vital to life.

11.
That discovery led to the second mission.

12.
The probe landed safely!

# Going for the Gold

Name _____ Date _____

Circle each adjective in the story.
Write each adjective and the noun it describes on the lines.
The first one has been done for you.

Gwen swung the (heavy) pick. The pick smashed down on the shiny rock. Gwen squealed as tiny bits broke away from the rock. Glen grabbed the flaky golden pieces. Gwen dropped the pick and aimed her flashlight beam at the rocks. Glen studied the glimmering fragments.

"Do you think it's real gold?" Gwen asked.

Glen scraped a rock along a gray boulder. The rock left a black streak.

"It's not actual gold," Glen sighed. "Gold leaves a yellow streak."

Next, Gwen chose a massive brown rock. She swung the awkward pick against the huge rock. It shattered. Sparkling yellow nuggets covered the dusty ground. Gwen and Glen picked up the glistening lumps. They each scraped a gleaming chunk along the rocky wall. As they stared at the yellow streaks on the wall, the astonished miners shouted, "Gold!"

| | Adjective | Noun | | | Adjective | Noun |
|---|---|---|---|---|---|---|
| 1. | heavy | pick | | 13. | | |
| 2. | | | | 14. | | |
| 3. | | | | 15. | | |
| 4. | | | | 16. | | |
| 5. | | | | 17. | | |
| 6. | | | | 18. | | |
| 7. | | | | 19. | | |
| 8. | | | | 20. | | |
| 9. | | | | 21. | | |
| 10. | | | | 22. | | |
| 11. | | | | 23. | | |
| 12. | | | | 24. | | |

# Bug Break

Name _____ Date _____

Write three adjectives that describe each bug.

**butterfly**
1. _____
2. _____
3. _____

**caterpillar**
4. _____
5. _____
6. _____

**beetle**
10. _____
11. _____
12. _____

**ladybug**
7. _____
8. _____
9. _____

**ant**
13. _____
14. _____
15. _____

Choose three of the bugs to write sentences about.
Use two adjectives in each sentence.

16. _____

_____

17. _____

_____

18. _____

_____

Adjectives that tell what kind

# Lake Hunt

Name _____  Date _____

Circle each adjective that tells how many.
Connect the circled words to show the path to the lake.

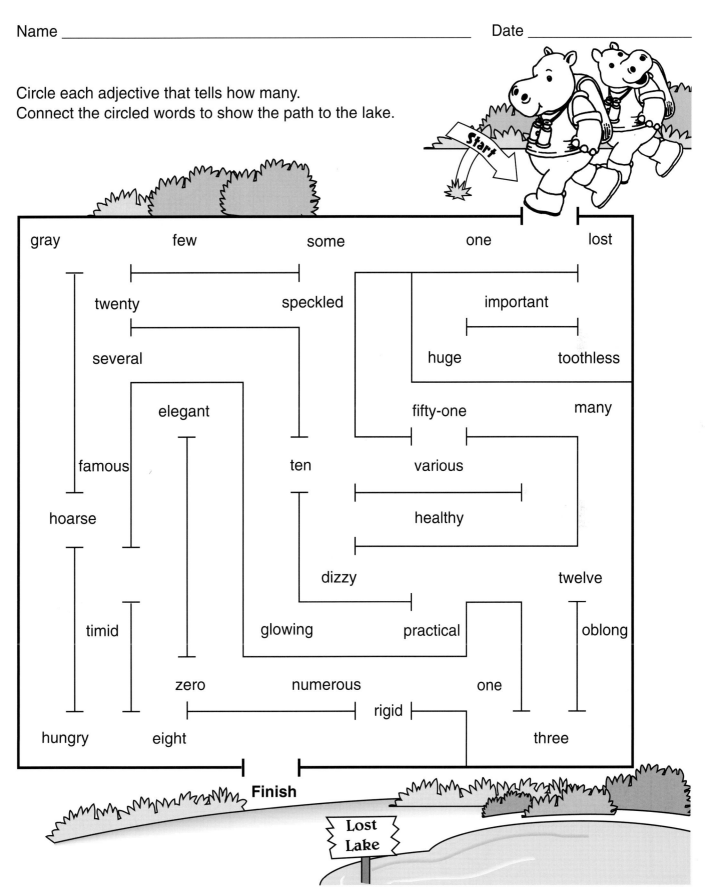

gray      few      some      one      lost

twenty      speckled      important

several      huge      toothless

elegant      fifty-one      many

famous      ten      various

hoarse      healthy

timid      dizzy      twelve

glowing      practical      oblong

zero      numerous      one

rigid

hungry      eight      three

**Finish**

**Lost Lake**

# Champion Cereals

Name _____    Date _____

Circle each adjective on the cereal boxes.
Write each adjective on the lines below.

Golden Flakes
With
Real Honey
Sixteen Ounces

WHEAT
SQUARES

Nine Vitamins
Whole Wheat

Oat Crunchies
Frosted Bites
Lowfat

Five New
Varieties

Wholesome
Apple
Bites
Ten Ounces

Honey Nut Flakes
Sweet Treat

Free Spoon

One Gram Of Sugar

Crunchy Rice
Perfect Snack
Eleven Vitamins
Twelve Ounces

## Adjectives That Tell
## How Many

_____

_____

_____

_____

_____

_____

## Adjectives That Tell
## What Kind

_____    _____

_____    _____

_____    _____

_____    _____

_____    _____

_____    _____

# "Bee-MX"

Name _____     Date _____

Color the correct adjective to show the path to the trophy.

1. Ben's old bike was the _____ motocross bike made.
2. The small bike was made for a much _____ rider.
3. Ben's new bike has a very _____ frame.
4. Even though it's light, the new bike's frame is _____.
5. The tires are _____ than regular bike tires.
6. Ben's new bike is one of the _____ bikes you can buy.
7. Ben rides this bike on _____ courses than before.
8. This bike is _____ than Ben's old bike.
9. Ben saved his allowance for _____ than two years.
10. Saving money was the _____ thing Ben had ever done.
11. Ben's bike is the _____ thing he has ever bought.
12. At his first race, Ben was _____ than he thought he'd be.
13. He was _____ by the second race.
14. Now Ben thinks racing is much _____.
15. He is the _____ rider on the course.

| small | smaller | smallest |
| young | younger | youngest |
| light | lighter | lightest |
| strong | stronger | strongest |
| wide | wider | widest |
| tough | tougher | toughest |
| rough | rougher | roughest |
| valuable | more valuable | most valuable |
| long | longer | longest |
| hard | harder | hardest |
| good | better | best |
| nervous | more nervous | most nervous |
| brave | braver | bravest |
| fun | more fun | most fun |
| happy | happier | happiest |

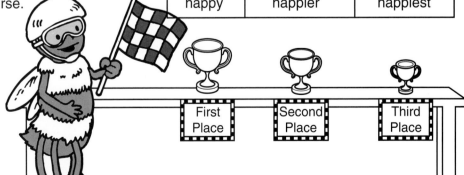

First Place     Second Place     Third Place

# Jazz It Up!

Name _____   Date _____

Complete the chart with the correct adjectives.
The first one has been done for you.

| Positive | Comparative | Superlative |
|----------|-------------|-------------|
| good | better | best |
| sad | | |
| | | prettiest |
| | sweeter | |
| fast | | |
| | | sharpest |
| | sillier | |
| busy | | |
| | worse | |
| many | | |
| | | most beautiful |
| | more difficult | |
| memorable | | |
| | | most popular |
| famous | | |

Write three sentences about your favorite music.
Use two different adjectives in each sentence.

1. _____

2. _____

3. _____

# Quilting Lesson

Circle each adverb.
Draw an arrow to the verb it describes.
Color by the code.

**Color Code**
tells when or where = orange
tells how = yellow

1. Buy cloth first.

2. Draw precisely.

3. Slowly trace.

4. Learn eagerly.

5. Then arrange the pieces.

6. Cut the cloth before you sew.

7. Never hurry.

8. Cut each piece carefully.

9. Work slowly.

10. Sew a seam there.

11. Talk sometimes.

12. Stuff cotton inside.

13. Work quietly.

14. Quilt skillfully.

15. Proudly spread the quilt.

16. Finally, you are finished.

# Looking for Lunch

Name _____ Date _____

Use an adverb or adverbs from the word
    bank to complete each sentence.
Use each adverb only once.

1. Leo darted _____ quickly over
   the _____ hot sand and rocks.

2. An _____ thorny tumbleweed
   rolled by.

3. The wind _____ suddenly picked
   up tiny bits of sand.

4. Leo _____ swiftly snuck up on
   a _____ lazy beetle.

5. Leo rolled out his _____ sticky tongue.

6. The _____ sneaky beetle sped away.

7. It had been _____ long since Leo's
   last meal.

8. Leo was _____ sad and
   _____ hungry.

9. He quietly looked around for a
   _____ sneaky bug.

10. Leo was _____ hopeful
    that a _____ slower bug
    was in his future.

## Word Bank

| | | |
|---|---|---|
| far | less | super |
| overly | fairly | extra |
| very | really | awfully |
| extremely | too | always |
| terribly | rather | much |
| somewhat | most | |
| quite | so | |

## Add words as directed to finish the poem about Leo.

Leo

_____   _____
adverb          adjective

_____
noun

_____   _____
adverb          adverb

_____
verb

Leo

# Comfortable?

Name _____ Date _____

Follow the steps to change each adjective into an adverb.
If the adverb tells how, mark an X in the how column.
If the adverb tells when, mark an X in the when column.

| How | When |
|-----|------|
| T | D |
| O | C |
| I | N |
| A | G |
| H | E |
| S | N |
| R | D |
| U | I |
| L | H |
| M | A |
| O | K |
| J | F |
| A | P |
| Q | E |
| R | V |
| W | T |
| Y | I |
| C | L |

1. loud + ly = _____
2. late + ly = _____
3. wild + ly = _____
4. quiet + ly = _____
5. day – y + i + ly = _____
6. quick + ly = _____
7. final + ly = _____
8. easy – y + i + ly = _____
9. slow + ly = _____
10. hungry – y + i + ly = _____
11. sudden + ly = _____
12. graceful + ly = _____
13. eventual + ly = _____
14. eager + ly = _____
15. immediate + ly = _____
16. full – l + ly = _____
17. clumsy – y + i + ly = _____
18. frequent + ly = _____

## What should you do if you find an elephant sitting in your chair?
To solve the riddle, match each letter that is not crossed out to the numbered lines below.

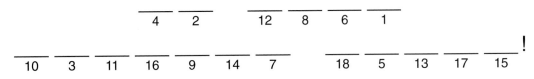

___ ___   ___ ___ ___ ___
4  2      12  8  6  1

___ ___ ___ ___ ___ ___ ___   ___ ___ ___ ___ ___!
10  3  11  16  9  14  7      18  5  13  17  15

# Bat Skateboarding!

Name _____     Date _____

Circle the word that each underlined adverb tells about.

1. Brett <u>excitedly</u> grabbed his new skateboard and gear.

2. He <u>quickly</u> strapped on the <u>very</u> shiny helmet.

3. Brett <u>proudly</u> spun each wheel.

4. Brett <u>promptly</u> put the skateboard <u>down</u>.

5. He <u>gently</u> placed one foot on the board.

6. He put the other foot <u>firmly</u> on the ground.

7. Brett <u>finally</u> pushed <u>off</u>.

8. He was <u>soon</u> gliding <u>skillfully</u> along.

9. Brett looked <u>quite</u> happy with his new board.

Rewrite each sentence, adding an adverb to tell more about each underlined word.

10. Brett <u>wanted</u> to jump the curb.

_____

11. He <u>pushed</u> off to get speed.

_____

12. Brett <u>crouched</u>.

_____

13. He <u>jumped</u> and <u>kicked</u>.

_____

14. Brett <u>crashed</u>, but he was <u>okay</u>.

_____

15. He <u>decided</u> to <u>try</u> again.

_____

# "Top-Knot-ch"

Name _____  Date _____

Color the knot with the correct adverb.

1. Nita entered the knot-tying contest _____ than Netty.

2. But Netty practiced _____ than Nita.

3. Nita thinks she'll win since she ties knots the _____ of all.

4. Netty ties knots _____ than Nita.

5. Netty hopes she'll win because her knots hold the _____ of all.

| early C | earlier O | earliest A |
| long E | longer N | longest D |
| fast I | faster G | fastest O |
| slowly B | more slowly A | most slowly J |
| well L | better F | best N |

| hard H | harder K | hardest N |
| little O | less I | least R |
| much V | more T | most O |
| badly A | worse W | worst P |
| often M | more often T | most often H |

6. Nita and Netty are working really _____.

7. They both like tying square knots _____ than other knots.

8. Nita says it's the _____ boring knot.

9. Netty feels she ties the square knot quite _____.

10. Netty wins contests _____ than Nita.

| quickly X | more quickly N | most quickly S |
| carefully U | more carefully Q | most carefully G |
| late I | later Y | latest K |

11. Nita ties ten knots _____ than Netty.

12. In contests, Netty ties square knots the _____ of all.

13. Netty finished tying ten knots the _____ of all, but she won!

### What did the knot say after it got tangled?
To answer the riddle, match the colored letters above to the numbered lines below.

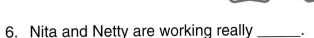
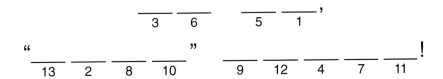

$$\underline{\phantom{xx}}\ \underline{\phantom{xx}}\ \underline{\phantom{xx}}\ \underline{\phantom{xx}},$$
3  6     5  1

"$\underline{\phantom{xx}}\ \underline{\phantom{xx}}\ \underline{\phantom{xx}}\ \underline{\phantom{xx}}$"  $\underline{\phantom{xx}}\ \underline{\phantom{xx}}\ \underline{\phantom{xx}}\ \underline{\phantom{xx}}\ \underline{\phantom{xx}}$!
13  2   8   10       9   12   4   7   11

Adverbs that compare  **75**

# Oasis Bound!

Name _____ Date _____

If the bold adverb is used correctly, color the shape to show the path to the oasis.
If the bold adverb is not used correctly, cross it out.
Write the correct adverb above it.

**Start**

1.
Cami
drives **straighter**
than Mel.

2.
Mel likes
desert driving
**good** than Cami.

3.
Mel
drives **much** in
the desert than in the city.

4.
Of all
Mel's friends,
Cami drives the **worst.**

5.
Mel handles
the desert sand
**better** than Cami does.

6.
Cami
likes desert
driving **least** than Mel.

7.
Mel finds
new roads **more
often** in the desert
than the city.

8.
Mel
drives **more
careful** on new roads.

9.
Cami likes
familiar roads
**well** than new ones.

10.
Cami
drives **well**
on city roads.

11.
Mel
drives **alert**
over sand dunes.

12.
For Mel,
coming down is
**most exciting** than
going up.

13.
The blowing
sand **badly** affects
what Mel can see.

14.
Cami and
Mel get to the oasis
before the wind gets **worse.**

**Finish**

Adverbs that compare

# Tuba Trouble

Name _____  Date _____

Circle the conjunction in each sentence.

1. Toby knew he had a concert; however, it wasn't until later.
2. He thought he'd go eat dinner since he was ready early.
3. Toby meant to stay clean, but something went wrong.
4. He was being careful while he ate a salad.
5. Toby had napkins, napkins, and more napkins.
6. He hoped that he wouldn't spill anything.
7. He wasn't worried, though the time was slipping away.
8. Before he knew what had happened, Toby's salad was in his lap.
9. He just watched as a waiter stumbled into his table.
10. He saw the salad bowl flying, yet he couldn't stop it.
11. Toby was in trouble, for dressing-coated lettuce dripped down his suit.
12. Toby would have to change or perform in a salad suit.
13. After he paid his bill, Toby jumped up.
14. He was being less careful than he should have been.
15. Because he jumped up too fast, Toby knocked over a bowl of gravy.
16. Toby was coated in food, so he dashed toward the door.
17. He had less than one hour until he had to be on stage.
18. Toby was headed to change when he remembered he only had one suit.

## How do you clean a dirty tuba?
To find out, write each conjunction in the puzzle below.

# Carry On!

Name _____ Date _____

Choose a conjunction pair from the rocks to complete each sentence.

1. _____ are ants strong, _____some can also carry things 20 times as heavy as they are.
2. _____ it's a cookie crumb _____ a piece of candy, the sugar ant will carry it off.
3. Ants often carry _____ bits of food _____ ant eggs.
4. Ants might carry eggs _____ inside their own nests _____ to their nest, from other nests.
5. Ants use their jaws to carry what they need _____ it's food, rocks, _____ other ants.
6. Worker ants use _____ their jaws _____ their claws to dig tunnels.
7. The workers leave the rocks _____ near their entry _____ scatter them around.
8. Some ants' pointed jaws mean they can _____ carry _____ dig.
9. These ants need other ants to _____ take care of their nests _____ feed them.
10. Some ants _____ attack other nests, _____ they also carry the young ants away.
11. _____ they know it _____ not, ants help farmers.
12. Ants _____ control harmful insects _____ break up the soil with their tunnels.

both, and

whether, or

either, or

whether, or

both, and

both, and

either, or

neither, nor

not only, but

not only, but

both, and

whether, or

Choose three conjunction pairs. Write a sentence using each pair on the lines below.

13. _____

_____

14. _____

_____

15. _____

_____

# "Moose-ic" Lovers

Name _____ Date _____

Circle each pronoun.
Draw a box around its antecedent.

Hint: The **antecedent** is the noun or nouns that the pronoun replaces.

1. Marvin said that he was going to buy a new CD.

2. Molly heard and told Marvin to borrow hers.

3. Marcy insisted that she borrow the CD next.

4. Marvin dropped the CD case and it broke.

5. Molly picked up the pieces and threw them away.

6. Molly asked Marvin to be more careful with her CDs.

7. The friends grabbed their money and went shopping.

8. The clerk heard Marvin talking to himself.

9. Marvin giggled and continued his shopping.

10. Marcy bought herself two new CDs.

11. Marvin paid for a CD and began listening to it.

12. Marcy and Marvin spent hours playing their music.

13. Marvin was very happy with his music choice.

14. Marcy didn't like one CD and wanted to return it.

15. Molly told Marcy that she would buy the CD.

# Peppery Pups

Name _____ Date _____

Color the pronouns by the code.

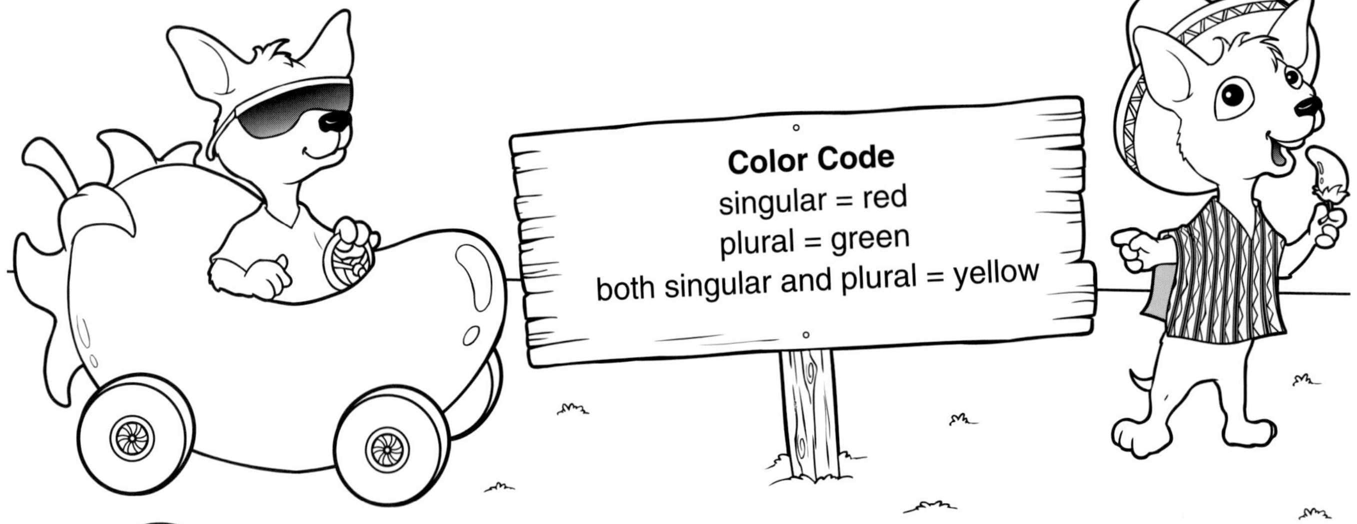

**Color Code**
singular = red
plural = green
both singular and plural = yellow

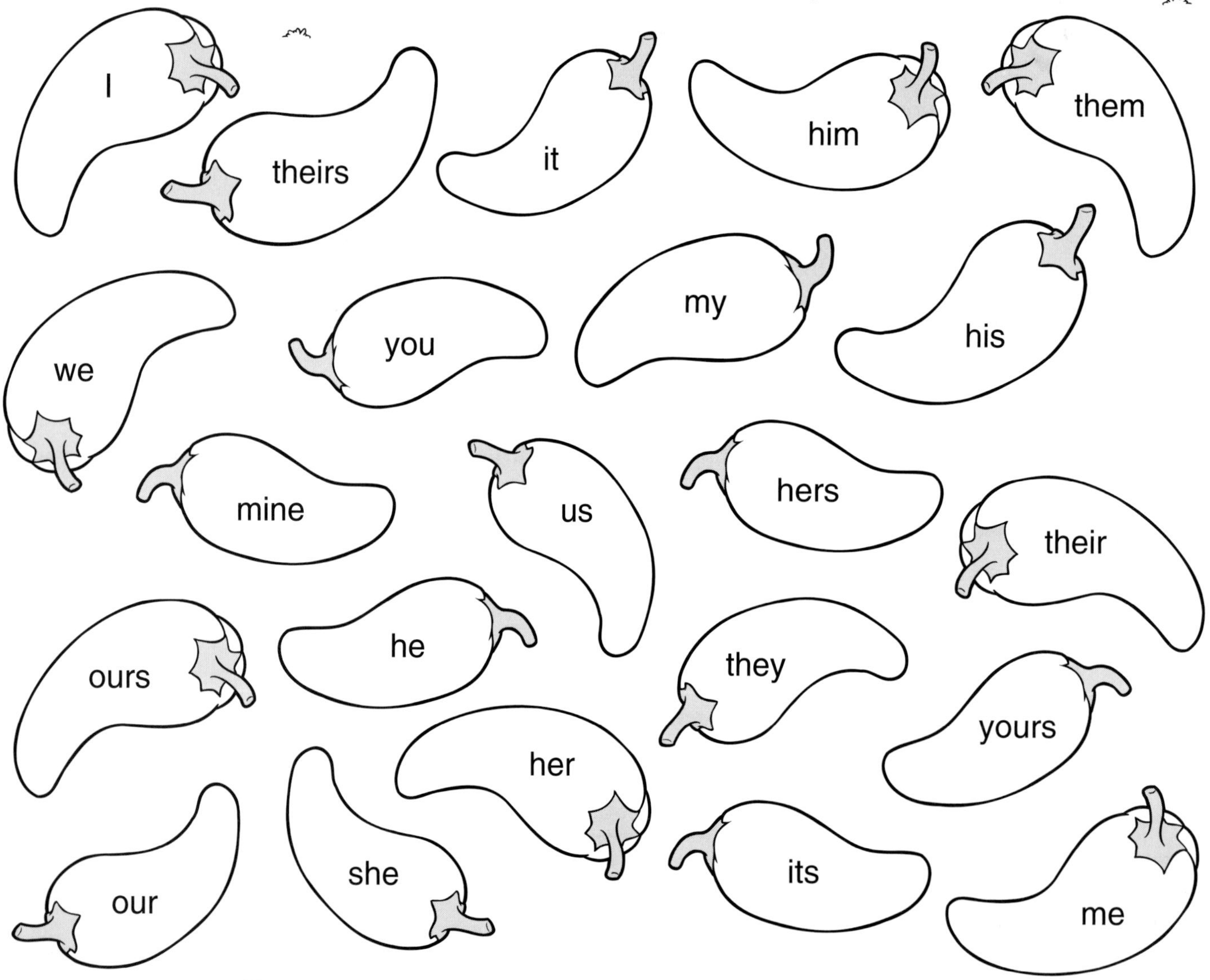

I

theirs

it

him

them

we

you

my

his

mine

us

hers

their

ours

he

they

yours

our

her

she

its

me

**pronouns: singular, plural**

# Peanutty Possessions

Name _____ Date _____

Write the correct possessive pronoun in each blank.
Cross off each pronoun that you use.
Some of the pronouns will not be crossed off.

**Possessive Pronouns Used Before a Noun**

my
your
its
her
his
our
their

1. Those unshelled peanuts belong to me.
   They are _____ peanuts.

2. That shelled bag of peanuts belongs to Paula.
   It is _____ bag.

3. Patty's peanuts and Penny's peanuts are warm.
   _____ peanuts are warm.

**Possessive Pronouns Used Alone**

mine
yours
his
hers
ours
theirs
its

4. Page's bag of peanuts weighs five pounds.
   _____ weight is five pounds.

5. Do those salted peanuts belong to you?
   Are those salted peanuts _____?

6. The honey-roasted peanuts belong to Pat and Pam.
   The honey-roasted peanuts are _____.

7. I bought these dry-roasted peanuts.
   These dry-roasted peanuts are _____.

8. The chocolate-covered peanuts are Paul's.
   The chocolate-covered peanuts are _____ .

9. We bought these unsalted peanuts.
   These are _____ unsalted peanuts.

10. The toffee-covered peanuts belong to Peter's mom.
    The toffee-covered peanuts are _____ mom's.

11. Does the bag of peanuts on the bench belong to you?
    Is it _____ bag?

12. The peanuts on the cart belong to Pat and me.
    The peanuts on the cart are _____.

# Good Ol' Granny Goose

Name _____ Date _____

Complete each sentence using either the pronoun *I* or *me*.
Color a matching pin for each pronoun you add.

1. Granny Goose saved the day for Gus and _____ !

2. It all started when Gus and _____ were riding bikes.

3. Of course, Gus and _____ were wearing our racing shirts.

4. We rode to the hill that Gus and _____ like to speed down.

6. Gus and _____ couldn't turn down a race!

5. Greg saw Gus and _____ there and wanted to race.

7. He would race both Gus and _____ .

8. As we raced, something knocked Gus and _____ off course.

9. Greg, Gus, and _____ all crashed!

10. The bikes landed on top of Greg and _____ .

11. Gus and _____ had torn our racing shirts.

12. Later, Granny saw Gus and _____ looking sad.

13. Gus and _____ cheered when Granny had sewn our shirts.

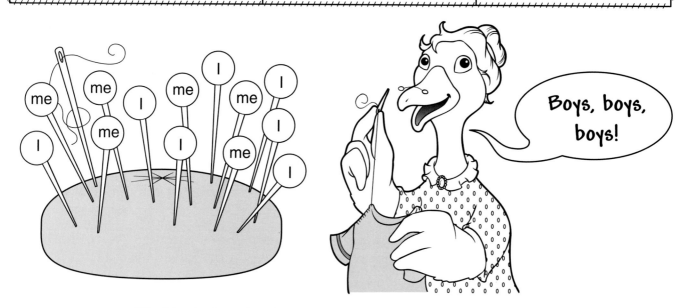

Boys, boys, boys!

# It's a Ten!

Choose an interjection from the word bank to complete each sentence below.

**Word Bank**

Oh
Hey
Oh my
Oh no
Ouch
Well
Wow
Yikes
Rats
Hooray
Yippee
Gadzooks
Good grief
My goodness

1. ___ ___ _w_ ! This is my first diving meet.

2. ___ ___   ___ ___ ___ (___) _e_ ___ ___ , is that a hot tub?

3. ___ ___ (___) _s_ ! We missed the first driver.

4. ___ (___) _e_ ___ ! That diver made a huge splash.

5. ___ (___)   ___ _o_ , the score will be low.

6. ___ (___) ___ ___ ___ ___ ___ _s_ ! How does a diver dry off with that tiny towel?

7. (___) _e_ ___ ! That diver hardly made a splash.

8. ___ ___ , so it is possible to score ten points.

9. ___ ___ ___ (___) _a_ ___ ! That's another diver who didn't really splash.

10. ___ ___ _c_ ___ ! That dive looked like it hurt.

11. ___ ___ ___ (___)   ___ ___ _i_ ___ ___ , the diving board is really high.

12. ___ (___) ___ ___ ___ _e_ ! That was the best dive I've seen.

13. ___ ___   ___ _y_ ! I like the way this diver jumps.

14. ___ (___) ___ _l_ , a diving meet is soggy, but it's fun.

## Where do seals watch movies?

To solve the riddle, match the circled letters to the numbered lines below.

___ ___ ___  " ___ ___ _v_ ___ - ___ ___ "
3  7  14        11  12      14    4   2

___ ___ ___ ___ ___ ___ ___
3  5  14  6  3  14  9

# What's Cooking?

Name _____ Date _____

Use the words to write a sentence
   that has an interjection.
Use correct punctuation
   and capitalization.

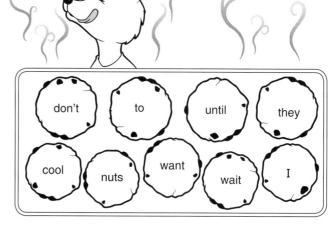

chocolate  smell  wow  chip  those  great  cookies

don't  to  until  they  cool  nuts  want  wait  I

1. _____

2. _____

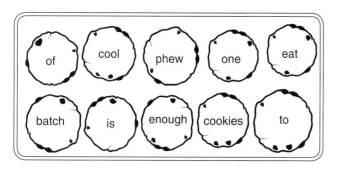

of  cool  phew  one  eat  batch  is  enough  cookies  to

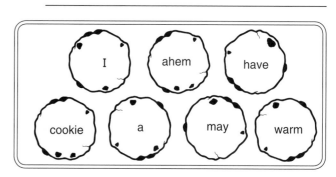

I  ahem  have  cookie  a  may  warm

3. _____

4. _____

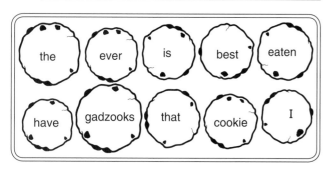

the  ever  is  best  eaten  have  gadzooks  that  cookie  I

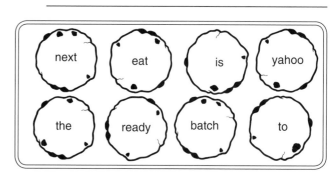

next  eat  is  yahoo  the  ready  batch  to

5. _____

6. _____

# Peppy Paula

Name _____ Date _____

Underline the 15 prepositions in the poem.
Decide what each preposition tells.
Write the preposition on the correct leaf.
The first one has been done for you.

**Location**
(where something is)

in _____ _____ _____

_____ _____ _____

**Direction**
(where something is going)

_____ _____

_____ _____

**Time**
(when something
happens)

_____

_____

_____

_____

**Relationship**
(a connection between a noun
and another word)

_____

Paula the parrot lives <u>in</u> a tree
On an island within the deep blue sea.
She never sleeps during the day.
She sleeps at night, so people say.

She wakes at dawn and flies toward the West
Past big ships and then back to her nest.
After a rest, she is back in the air
And flying again without a care.

She waves to a friend walking along the beach;
Then she says goodbye with a very loud screech.

Finish the poem, using at least one preposition in each line.

_____

_____

# A "Moo-velous" Party

Name _____   Date _____

Underline the 25 prepositional phrases on the invitation.
Circle each preposition.
Write a response on the card shown that includes two prepositional phrases.

### Invitation for Clem

Come to Clara's party!

The party will start at 1 P.M. on Saturday.

Clowns from Clark's Clown School will perform in
   a circle around the guests.

After the clowns' show, we'll watch the movie
   *Pastures of Clover.*

During the movie, we'll munch on hay cakes and sip
   from punch glasses.

We'll go down the hill and play games until 4 P.M.

Then we'll eat ice cream topped with oat sprinkles.

Before the party ends, we'll walk across the pasture.

And we'll dance inside the barn until dark.

It will be a great party among friends!

Without you at the party, I'll be sad.

I hope I hear from you soon!

Clara

RSVP by Friday at noon.

Response Card

# Polar Picture

Name _____  Date _____

For 1–9, write a prepositional phrase telling where each animal or thing is.
For 10–12, write a prepositional phrase telling where each animal is moving.
Cross off a preposition on the frame after you use it.
The first one has been done for you.

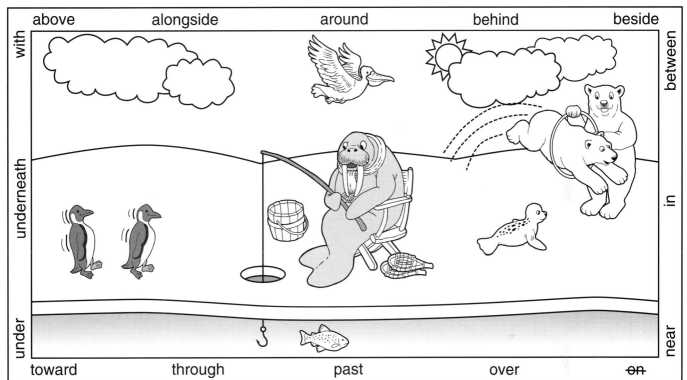

1. chair _on the ice_____

2. fish _____

3. seal _____

4. sun _____

5. snowshoes _____

6. scarf _____

7. fishing line _____

8. pelican _____

9. pail _____

10. polar bear _____

11. penguin _____

12. fish _____

Write sentences about the picture using any two prepositional phrases you wrote above.

13. _____

14. _____

# Piggy Bank Problems

Name _____     Date _____

If the underlined words form a subject phrase, color the coin red.
If the underlined words form a predicate phrase, color the coin blue.

1.
<u>Peter and Paul</u> are piggy banks.

M

2.
People <u>store change in piggy banks</u>.

Y

3.
<u>Each piggy bank</u> holds lots of change.

N

4.
Paul <u>will save his money</u>.

I

5.
Peter <u>gives money away</u>.

A

6.
<u>The money</u> is running out.

E

7.
Peter <u>counts his money</u> every day.

D

8.
They both <u>want a coin collection</u>.

J

9.
<u>All their friends</u> are wealthy.

Y

10.
Peter and Paul <u>visited the bank</u>.

R

11.
<u>A coin collection</u> was on display.

T

12.
<u>The silver coins</u> were Paul's favorite.

A

13.
Peter <u>saved money for weeks</u>.

N

14.
<u>The two friends</u> bought a coin collection.

K

SHHH!

## Why can't the piggy bank sleep at night?
To solve the riddle, write the boldfaced letters from the red-colored coins in order on the lines below.

Because ____ O ____ ____ ____

____ ____ L ____ S !

©The Education Center, Inc. • *Target Reading & Writing Success* • TEC60875 • Key p. 133

**Sentences: subjects and predicates**

# Sheep Dreams

Name _____ Date _____

Underline the compound subject or compound predicate in each sentence.
Color a matching sheep for each one you underline.

predicate  predicate  predicate  predicate  predicate  predicate

predicate

predicate

predicate

1. Mom and dad told Sherman to go to bed.

2. Sherman combed and brushed his coat.

3. Then he yawned and climbed into bed.

4. Sherman turned over and tried to sleep.

5. He relaxed and counted sheep.

6. Then Sherman slept and dreamt about a shearing contest.

7. Sherman and Shelly wanted to win first prize.

8. Shelly and Sherman are best friends.

9. The friends and their parents went to the shearing room.

10. The sheep were proudly sheared and clipped.

11. All the sheep gathered and listened to hear the contest winner.

12. They watched and waited while the farmer filled a feedbox.

13. Sherman and Shelly were announced as the contest winners!

14. The other sheep shouted and cheered.

15. Sherman and Shelly couldn't believe their ears.

subject

subject

subject

subject

subject

**Sentences: compound subjects and predicates**

# Mole Matters

Name _____ Date _____

If the sentence is simple, mark an X under the simple column.
If the sentence is compound, mark an X under the compound column.

Finish

| Simple | Compound | |
|---|---|---|
| P | M | 1. Moles are small creatures that live underground. |
| Y | E | 2. Moles are nearly blind, but they hear well. |
| I | R | 3. They are tireless diggers, and they love to dig tunnels. |
| S | A | 4. Three moles are racing through an underground maze. |
| W | J | 5. Maggie is small, but she is very fast. |
| N | A | 6. Her brother Mason is tall and skinny. |
| M | T | 7. Mary is the oldest, but she is also the shortest. |
| L | E | 8. Mason and Mary are in first place. |
| Z | C | 9. Maggie isn't far behind, and she's closing in. |
| H | R | 10. All three moles are close to the finish line. |
| A | U | 11. Now they are all even, but each one wants to get ahead. |
| K | I | 12. Mason has moved to the front, and he's leading the race. |
| B | D | 13. Both of his sisters are trying hard to catch up with him. |
| C | V | 14. Maggie has caught up with him, and she's in first place! |
| G | S | 15. Maggie won the race, and she received the winner's trophy. |

## What did Maggie say about winning the underground race?
To find out, match the letters that are not crossed to the numbered lines below.

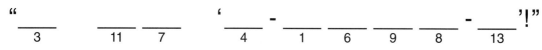

" ___ ___ ___ ' ___ - ___ ___ ___ ___ - ___ '!"
   3     11   7     4    1   6   9   8   13

**Sentences: simple and compound**

# Camping Out

Name _____  Date _____

Decide whether each group of words is a fragment, a sentence, or a run-on.
Write the sentence number on a matching campfire rock.

1. Camping can be a lot of fun.

2. People camp in many places they camp all over the world.

3. In mountains, valleys, and near rivers.

4. Some people camp in tents other people camp in RVs.

5. Campers should plan their trips ahead of time.

6. Planning helps make sure campers are safe and prepared.

7. You don't need a lot of gear to have fun camping.

8. You comfortable place to sleep.

9. Some people prefer to camp in a tent they feel closer to nature.

10. Plus, cheaper than RVs.

11. Sleeping bag, warm clothing, food, and other equipment.

12. Campers should always carry a first aid kit.

Fragment          Sentence          Run-on

**Sentences: complete and incomplete**  91

# Hamster Hop

Name _____ Date _____

Form a compound sentence by combining the two sentences shown
    for each pair of jukebox buttons.

| A | He asked her to dance. | 1 | His wife likes rap. |
| B | Hannah got new shoes. | 2 | They hurt her feet. |
| C | Holly loves to dance. | 3 | We could get a burger. |
| D | Harry likes country music. | 4 | She said she would like to. |
| E | We could dance. | 5 | I have no money. |
| F | I'd like to get a burger. | 6 | Henry wore a black suit. |
| G | Hal likes jazz. | 7 | She dances to every song. |
| H | Henry's date wore a red dress. | 8 | His sister loves rock and roll. |

A  4  _____

B  2  _____

C  7  _____

D  1  _____

E  3  _____

F  5  _____

_____

G  8  _____

_____

H  6  _____

_____

Sentences: compound sentences

# High Flyers

Name _____   Date _____

Use each sentence fragment to write a complete sentence on the line.

1. loves flying kites

2. the hot sun beating down

3. went to the park

4. not my favorite kite

5. soaring and flying high

6. huge gust of wind

7. tangled lines in the trees

8. felt very glad

1. _____

2. _____

3. _____

4. _____

5. _____

6. _____

7. _____

8. _____

# A Passion for Peanuts

Name _____  Date _____

Fix each run-on sentence by forming two complete sentences.

1. One day I walked into the kitchen I immediately started to smile.

1A _____

1B _____
_____

2. I saw a pile of peanuts on a table they looked so tasty.

2A _____

2B _____
_____

3. There was a sign in front of the peanuts the sign had my name on it.

3A _____

3B _____
_____

4. I realized the peanuts were all for me I quickly started eating them.

4A _____

4B _____
_____

5. I ate the peanuts so quickly I got a bellyache I had to go to the doctor.

5A _____

5B _____
_____

6. That's when I stopped eating peanuts the next time I got peanuts, I gave them away.

6A _____

6B _____
_____

**Sentences: run-ons**

# Banned Bulls

Name _____ Date _____

Circle the correct verb to complete the sentence.

1. Ms. Smith (own, owns) a nice little china shop.

2. The shop (has, have) great products.

3. She (sell, sells) many types of cups, plates, and vases.

4. Hundreds of people (shop, shops) there each day.

5. Many store owners (allow, allows) animals in their stores.

6. Ms. Smith (frown, frowns) upon animals in her store.

7. She no longer (grant, grants) them permission to enter.

8. People still (recall, recalls) the day a bull came in and broke all the china.

9. The animals (know, knows) not to go inside the shop.

10. They (wait, waits) outside until their owners are finished shopping.

Select four verbs that you did not circle and write each one in a plate.
Then write a sentence for each verb you chose.

_____

_____

_____

_____

Sentences: subject-verb agreement 95

# Homeward Bound

Name _____     Date _____

Color the star beside the correct word to complete the sentence.

| | | | | | | |
|---|---|---|---|---|---|---|
| 1. | Hi, my name _____ Connie Constellation. | E | is | R | are |
| 2. | I _____ on my way home. | G | am | I | are |
| 3. | My family _____ on a planet far away. | K | live | M | lives |
| 4. | It _____ me about ten light years to get there. | S | take | R | takes |
| 5. | I _____ being here on Earth. | E | love | N | loves |
| 6. | I _____ many new friends when I visit. | L | meets | D | meet |
| 7. | My new friend, Mark, _____ to visit me someday. | P | want | E | wants |
| 8. | He _____ to bring his family along. | O | hopes | Y | hope |
| 9. | My favorite food on Earth _____ pizza. | S | is | W | are |
| 10. | It _____ the best thing I've ever tasted! | P | is | H | are |
| 11. | My family _____ to try some pizza too. | C | hopes | T | hope |
| 12. | They _____ to try new foods! | X | love | F | loves |
| 13. | My parents and sisters _____ waiting for me to come home. | A | is | V | are |
| 14. | I've packed everything, and I _____ ready to take off. | S | am | B | is |
| 15. | The rocket engine _____ as I travel back home. | T | roars | G | roar |

## How did Connie get home?

To solve the riddle, match the letters from the colored stars to the numbered blanks below.

She rode the __ __ __ __ __
            11  8  3  5  15

__ __ __ __ __ __ __ !
1  12  10  4  7  14  9

I survived a trip to Earth!

# Cookie Munchers!

Name _____  Date _____

Decide whether the underlined words make up an independent clause or a dependent clause. Write the sentence number on a cookie in the matching cookie jar.

1. <u>Since I was late</u>, I ran four blocks to the cookie shop.

2. I was meeting Maggie there <u>because we both love cookies</u>.

3. Since I wasn't there, <u>Maggie ordered without me</u>.

4. She was eating a peanut butter cookie <u>that looked delicious</u>.

5. I ordered chocolate chip cookies <u>because they were on sale</u>.

6. <u>My order was less than a dollar</u> because of the sale.

7. <u>I wanted to save my money</u> so I could go to the movies.

8. I got my order quickly <u>since we were the only customers</u>.

9. Since I was starving, <u>I began to eat my cookie</u>.

10. Maggie started eating before me, <u>so she finished first</u>.

11. I tried to eat quickly <u>because the movie started soon</u>.

12. Because we were running late, <u>Maggie was in a hurry</u>.

13. <u>She put her coat on</u> when I was almost finished.

14. We hurried down the street <u>because the theater is ten blocks away</u>.

15. When we have to, <u>Maggie and I can run really fast</u>!

# Pillow Party

Name _____ Date _____

Form complex sentences by matching each independent clause with a dependent clause.
Write the numbers from both clauses in a feather.
Write the new sentence on the line.

1. which made me upset

2. I love having pillow fights

3. because the cover is thick

4. you hit me too hard

5. because they are fun

6. because it has a tear

7. my pillow isn't breaking

8. which we'll clean up

9. my pillow will break soon

10. the feathers will make a big mess

_____
_____

_____
_____

_____
_____

_____
_____

_____
_____

**Clauses: independent, dependent**

Parent Communication and Student Checkups

# Parent Communication and Student Checkups

## Table of Contents

### How to Administer the checkups

Both checkups can be given at the same time, or Checkup B can be given as a follow-up test for students who did not do well on Checkup A. The checkups will help you determine which students have mastered a skill and which students may need more practice.

# Student Progress Chart

| student | | Date | Number Correct | Comments |
|---|---|---|---|---|
| **Checkup 1** Capitalization | A | | | |
| | B | | | |
| **Checkup 2** Ending punctuation | A | | | |
| | B | | | |
| **Checkup 3** Commas | A | | | |
| | B | | | |
| **Checkup 4** Quotation marks | A | | | |
| | B | | | |
| **Checkup 5** Apostrophes | A | | | |
| | B | | | |
| **Checkup 6** Nouns | A | | | |
| | B | | | |
| **Checkup 7** Verbs | A | | | |
| | B | | | |
| **Checkup 8** Adjectives | A | | | |
| | B | | | |
| **Checkup 9** Adverbs | A | | | |
| | B | | | |
| **Checkup 10** Pronouns | A | | | |
| | B | | | |
| **Checkup 11** Sentences | A | | | |
| | B | | | |

# It's Time to Take Aim!

On _____ our class will be having a checkup on **capitalization.**
To help your child prepare, please spend about 15 minutes reviewing this skill.

## Skill Refresher

Hide the answers at the bottom of the page. Guide your child through the rules and examples below. Then have him complete problems 1–8.

- Capitalize the **first word in a sentence.**
  All of the students were present.

- Capitalize **proper nouns.**
  Dr. Jeanine Lutt       Steven A. Thomas
  Gold Auditorium       Empire State Building

- Capitalize the **days** of the week, **months** of the year, and **holidays.**
  Monday       January       Thanksgiving

- Capitalize **geographic names.**
  Earth       Baton Rouge       Appalachian Mountains

- Capitalize the **first word, last word,** and any **main words** in a **title.**
  *James and the Giant Peach*
  "This Land Is Your Land"

**Answers:**

1. Have you heard "Pop! Goes the Weasel" lately?
2. Tracy's family moved to Maryland last Thursday.
3. Sometimes my birthday is on Labor Day.
4. **Cindy's** all-time favorite book is *Little House on the Prairie.*
5. **Ms.** Jones has studied in England, France, and Greece.
6. The Great Lakes include Lake Huron and Lake Michigan.
7. **Dr.** Gale's office is located at 1602 South Windy Lane.
8. **Did** you read **Sunday's** comics in the *Daily News?*

©The Education Center, Inc. • *Target Reading & Writing Success* • TEC60875

## Target These!

Circle each letter that should be capitalized.

1. have you heard "pop! goes the weasel" lately?

2. tracy's family moved to maryland last thursday.

3. sometimes my birthday is on labor day.

4. cindy's all-time favorite book is *little house on the prairie.*

5. ms. jones has studied in england, france, and greece.

6. the great lakes include lake huron and lake michigan.

7. dr. gale's office is located at 1602 south windy lane.

8. did you read sunday's comics in the *daily news?*

# Checkup 1

Name _____ Date _____

Circle each letter that should be capitalized.

1. sally and sue both have birthdays in march right after st. patrick's day.

2. if you go to arizona, be sure to visit the grand canyon.

3. dr. tom gray is the dentist that i go to.

4. i gave mr. holman my report about the statue of liberty.

5. have you read *the computer nut* by betsy byars?

6. steph jackson lives just off the beach on long island.

7. todd, trish, and tony are going to raft down the green river.

8. the high school choir sang "the star-spangled banner" last night.

9. on saturday my cousin from florida will visit.

10. mr. gray is taking us on a field trip in may.

©The Education Center, Inc. • *Target Reading & Writing Success* • TEC60875 • Key p. 135

**Test A:** Capitalization

---

# Checkup 1

Name _____ Date _____

Circle each letter that should be capitalized.

1. the hulls always have a huge picnic on the fourth of july.

2. have you read the poem "paul revere's ride"?

3. mrs. crosby will be at smith hall on monday, thursday, and friday.

4. we crossed the great salt lake two times on our trip to utah.

5. joe studied the planet mars for his report on the milky way.

6. uncle john sang "row, row, row your boat" on the way to the lake.

7. alice's cousin anna moved here from peru.

8. we went to mount rushmore last june.

9. my favorite book is *hatchet* by gary paulsen.

10. we are having a test on the tuesday after easter.

©The Education Center, Inc. • *Target Reading & Writing Success* • TEC60875 • Key p. 135

**Test B:** Capitalization

# It's Time to Take Aim!

On _____ our class will be having a checkup on **ending punctuation**.
To help your child prepare, please spend about 15 minutes reviewing this skill.

## Skill Refresher

Hide the answers at the bottom of the page. Guide your child through the rules and examples below. Then have him complete problems 1–8.

- **A period** is used at the end of a sentence that makes a statement or gives a command.

  We are going swimming after lunch.

- **A question mark** is used at the end of a question.

  Have you seen my brother?

- **An exclamation mark** shows strong feeling.

  Wow, that home run was amazing!

### Target These!

Add the ending punctuation.

1. Orange is my favorite color

2. Where are your books

3. Wow, I made an A on my test

4. Who do these shoes belong to

5. I'm going to watch the game

6. Yippee, I can't wait to see him

7. I hope we get there soon

8. Can we get some ice cream

**Answers:**

1. Orange is my favorite color.
2. Where are your books?
3. Wow, I made an A on my test!
4. Who do these shoes belong to?
5. I'm going to watch the game.
6. Yippee, I can't wait to see him!
7. I hope we get there soon.
8. Can we get some ice cream?

# Checkup 2

Name _____   Date _____

Add the ending punctuation.

1. Pass the potatoes, please

2. Can I have some candy after dinner

3. Wow, I'm too excited to sit still

4. We have two dogs at my house

5. Where are we going now

6. Ouch, that hurt

7. Is there any pizza left from the party

8. My birthday is December 3

9. How are you feeling today

10. Can we go to the park tomorrow

# Checkup 2

Name _____   Date _____

Add the ending punctuation.

1. Where are the stickers that I gave you

2. I'll have a small soda, please

3. Watch out, or you'll fall off the edge

4. We have a soccer game tonight

5. I finished my homework after school

6. Let's wait for them to come home

7. Are those your pencils on the floor

8. Oh my, I got all As on my report card

9. Can I sit here next to you

10. I can't believe we won the championship

# It's Time to Take Aim!

On _____ our class will be having a checkup on **commas.**
To help your child prepare, please spend about 15 minutes reviewing this skill.

## Skill Refresher

Hide the answers at the bottom of the page. Guide your child through the rules and examples below. Then have him correctly punctuate sentences 1–7.

- Use commas to separate the **day** and the **year.** They also separate the **city** and the **state.**

  June 2, 2008     September 4, 1981
  Bangor, Maine     Boston, Massachusetts

- Use commas in letters after the **greeting** and **closing.**

  Dear Matt,          Sincerely,

- Use commas to separate an **introductory phrase** from the rest of the sentence.
  Yes, I'd like a piece of cake.

- Use commas to separate **items in a series.**
  We saw lions, tigers, and elephants at the zoo.

- Use commas to separate the **direct address noun** from the rest of the sentence.
  Ramon, please answer the phone.

- Use commas to separate **appositives** from the rest of the sentence.
  Jennifer, my sister, is 12 years old.

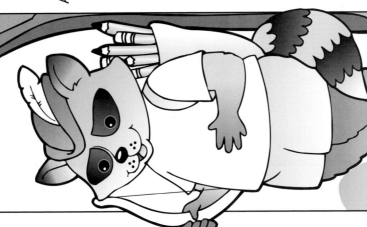

## Target These!

Add commas where needed.

1. That event happened on November 8 1868.

2. Our family is going to visit Orlando Florida.

3. Dear Mom
   I'm having a great time at Grandma's.
                    Your son
                    Steve

4. No we aren't going to the movies today.

5. I left my notebook homework and bookbag at school.

6. Leah you can go outside now.

7. Mrs. Smith my teacher loves to teach math.

**Answers:**

1. That event happened on November 8, 1868.

2. Our family is going to visit Orlando, Florida.

3. Dear Mom,
   I'm having a great time at Grandma's.
                    Your son,
                    Steve

4. No, we aren't going to the movies today.
5. I left my notebook, homework, and bookbag at school.
6. Leah, you can go outside now.
7. Mrs. Smith, my teacher, loves to teach math.

©The Education Center, Inc. • *Target Reading & Writing Success* • TEC60875

# Checkup 3

Name _____ Date _____

Add missing commas.

1. He was born on August 15 2001.

2. Jamie went to Las Vegas Nevada.

3. Dear Julie
   I hope to see you soon!
   Love
   Trey

4. No you can't borrow my skis.

5. I want a hamburger fries and a shake.

6. Pedro could I borrow a pencil?

7. Troy my classmate won the essay contest.

8. Well would you like to go to the game?

9. Turn in your paper Marcus.

10. I gave cards to my mom dad and sister.

---

# Checkup 3

Name _____ Date _____

Add missing commas.

1. Abraham Lincoln was born on February 12 1809.

2. I'm going to Denver Colorado.

3. My favorite foods are fruit cookies and sandwiches.

4. Dear Dad
   I'm having a great time at the beach!
   Your daughter
   Ellie

5. Sure you can use my phone.

6. Dena where are you going?

7. Mr. Davis my football coach is a great athlete.

8. Well did you find your homework?

9. My teacher Mr. Thomas knows a lot about history.

10. Running quickly I reached the finish line.

# It's Time to Take Aim!

On _____ our class will be having a checkup on **quotation marks**. To help your child prepare, please spend about 15 minutes reviewing this skill.

## Skill Refresher

Hide the answers at the bottom of the page. Guide your child through the rules and examples below. Then have him complete problems 1–8.

- Put **quotation marks** before and after a speaker's exact words. Use a **comma** to separate the speaker from the quoted words.

  Sam said, "Please shut the door."

- Place **commas and ending punctuation** inside the second set of quotation marks.

  Davis said, "What a beautiful dog!"
  "Where," asked Ted, "are we going?"

- **Capitalize** the first word in a quotation.

  Amy said, "Don't forget the butter."

## Target These!

Add quotation marks and commas where needed.

1. Jenny whined I've lost my shoes.
2. We won! John shouted.
3. I thought that we agreed not to get a dog Mom moaned.

If the sentence has a direct quote, add quotation marks and commas where needed.

4. Travis said that he wanted to come over after school.
5. There are too many choices Tina complained.
6. Be sure Ms. Hill said to bring back that folder.

Rewrite each sentence correctly on the back of this page.

7. "Coach said run three" laps to, warm up.
8. Did you read the comics today I asked?

**Answers:**

1. Jenny whined, **"**I've lost my shoes.**"**
2. **"**We won!**"** John shouted.
3. **"**I thought that we agreed not to get a dog,**"** Mom moaned.
4. indirect quotation
5. **"**There are too many choices,**"** Tina complained.
6. **"**Be sure,**"** Ms. Hill said, **"**to bring back that folder.**"**
7. Coach said, "Run three laps to warm up."
8. "Did you read the comics today?" I asked.

# Checkup 4

Name _____ Date _____

Add quotation marks, punctuation, and capital letters where needed.

1. Susan gushed I love that movie!

2. We're going to the water park Ellen said.

3. Hal asked can you come over?

4. Let's take the dog Amy begged and the cat too.

If the sentence has a direct quote, add quotation marks, commas, or capital letters where needed.

5. Phil walked three miles announced Dave.

6. Barb asked if I could go with her.

7. Carla said that she liked my bag.

8. Ms. Jones asked who is absent?

Rewrite each sentence correctly.

9. "There are, only two more cookies Gail" said.

10. Do you know how to divide asked Gary?

---

# Checkup 4

Name _____ Date _____

Add quotation marks, commas, and capital letters where needed.

1. Are you new? Paul asked.

2. There are two ways to get to school Jenny said.

3. Mr. Tony yelled we are out of pizza!

4. Have you heard Katy asked about this book?

If the sentence has a direct quote, add quotation marks and commas where needed.

5. Ms. Sands said that she wants us to work today.

6. I brought a cake Larry said.

7. Dana forgot her lunch Lucy told Janet.

8. Nita told us that she got a new puppy.

Rewrite each sentence correctly.

9. What time is "recess Tom asked"?

10. There is only "one way said Mary", to beat this puzzle.

# It's Time to Take Aim!

On _____ our class will be having a checkup on **apostrophes.**
To help your child prepare, please spend about 15 minutes reviewing this skill.

## Skill Refresher

Hide the answers at the bottom of the page. Guide your child through the rules and examples below. Then have him complete problems 1–10.

- Add **'s** to singular nouns to show ownership.

  Sandy**'s** shoes    kitten**'s** fur    tree**'s** leaves

- Add an apostrophe after a plural noun ending in s to show ownership.

  ladies' hats    chairs' legs    parents' cars

- Add **'s** to a plural noun that does not end in s to show ownership.

  geese**'s** food    children**'s** hats    sheep**'s** ears

- In a contraction an apostrophe takes the place of the missing letters.

  could not = couldn't    we have = we've    I am = I'm

## Target These!

Rewrite each phrase to show ownership.

1. car that belongs to Matt _____
2. pizza that belongs to Tina _____
3. dog that belongs to Larry _____
4. bikes that belong to boys _____
5. wings of birds _____
6. stems of flowers _____

Rewrite each word pair to make a contraction.

7. would not _____    8. he is _____

Write the words that form each contraction.

9. they've _____
10. we'll _____

**Answers:**

1. Matt's car
2. Tina's pizza
3. Larry's dog
4. boys' bikes
5. birds' wings
6. flowers' stems
7. wouldn't
8. he's
9. they have
10. we will

©The Education Center, Inc. • *Target Reading & Writing Success* • TEC60875

# Checkup 5

Name _____ Date _____

Rewrite each phrase to show ownership.

1. tail of a fox _____

2. cup that belongs to a child _____

3. paper that belongs to a student _____

4. manes of lions _____

5. erasers of pencils _____

6. headlines of newspapers _____

Rewrite each word pair to make a contraction.

7. was not _____   8. they are _____

9. we have _____   10. should not _____

Write the words that form each contraction.

11. here's _____   12. we're _____

13. you've _____   14. we've _____

**Test A:** Apostrophes

---

# Checkup 5

Name _____ Date _____

Rewrite each phrase to show ownership.

1. CD that belongs to Lynn _____

2. doll that belongs to Jasmine _____

3. baseball that belongs to Toby _____

4. screens of computers _____

5. children of parents _____

6. toys of dogs _____

Rewrite each word pair to make a contraction.

7. are not _____   8. could have _____

9. were not _____   10. they will _____

Write the words that form each contraction.

11. I'll _____   12. you're _____

13. don't _____   14. I've _____

**Test B:** Apostrophes

# It's Time to Take Aim!

On _____ our class will be having a checkup on **nouns.**
To help your child prepare, please spend about 15 minutes reviewing this skill.

## Skill Refresher

Hide the answers at the bottom of the page. Guide your child through the rules and examples below. Then have him complete problems 1–8.

- A **proper noun** names a special person, place, or thing.

  Mark Smith     England     Fourth of July

- Make a noun **plural** by adding **-s** or **-es** or by changing the **y** to **i** and adding **-es.**

  chai**rs**     beach**es**     penn**ies**

- A **possessive noun** shows to whom an item belongs.

  <u>singular possessive</u>     <u>plural possessive</u>
  Amy's dress                   dogs' leashes
  pencil's eraser               foxes' den

## Target These!

Circle the proper nouns.

1. Tuesday     boy     state
   New York City     food     Thomas

Make each noun singular or plural.

2. box      _____     tables
3. benches  _____     glass
4. candies  _____     bunny

Write whether each phrase is singular possessive or plural possessive.

5. watch's band
6. horses' saddles
7. girls' games
8. boy's parents

**Answers:**

1. Tuesday, New York City, Thomas
2. boxes, table
3. bench, glasses
4. candy, bunnies
5. singular possessive
6. plural possessive
7. plural possessive
8. singular possessive

112

©The Education Center, Inc. • *Target Reading & Writing Success* • TEC60875

# Checkup 6

Name _____ Date _____

Circle the proper nouns.

1. car     Texas     aunt

    November     Melissa     lemon

Make each noun singular or plural.

2. cities     _____     berry     _____

3. dresses     _____     sandwich     _____

4. bush     _____     potatoes     _____

Write whether each phrase is singular possessive or plural possessive.

5. Damon's radio _____

6. sisters' books _____

7. trees' branches _____

8. Maria's lunch _____

**Test A:** Nouns

---

# Checkup 6

Name _____ Date _____

Circle the proper nouns.

1. library     Mount Everest     Abraham Lincoln

    car wash     Brazil     grocery store

Make each noun singular or plural.

2. monkeys     _____     dish     _____

3. bunch     _____     menu     _____

4. valleys     _____     babies     _____

Write whether each phrase is singular possessive or plural possessive.

5. girls' birthdays _____

6. Juan's shoes _____

7. puppies' toys _____

8. man's coat _____

**Test B:** Nouns

# It's Time to Take Aim!

On _____ our class will be having a checkup on **verbs.**
To help your child prepare, please spend about 15 minutes reviewing this skill.

## Skill Refresher

Hide the answers at the bottom of the page. Guide your child through the rules and examples below. Then have him complete problems 1–10.

- An **action verb** tells what the subject is doing.
  The cat <u>jumped</u> onto the table.

- A **helping verb** helps express the tense of the main verb.
  We <u>should</u> go to the meeting.

- A **linking verb** links the subject to the word or words in the predicate.
  The dog <u>is</u> in his house.

- The **tense** of a verb tells when it takes place. The past tense of regular verbs is formed by adding -*ed*. The future tense of regular verbs is formed by using the helping verb *will* with the main verb.
  present: Terry <u>walks</u> to school every day.
  past:    Terry <u>walked</u> to school yesterday.
  future:  Terry <u>will walk</u> to school tomorrow.

- Some verbs are **irregular**. Their tenses are formed differently than regular verbs.
  present:         I like to <u>draw</u>.
  past:            I <u>drew</u> a picture.
  past participle: I <u>have drawn</u> a portrait.

## Target These!

Complete each sentence with an action verb from the box.

1. The dog _____ at the cat.
2. I _____ the ball to him.
3. She _____ for three hours.

| threw | barks | danced |

Circle the helping verb.

4. We have watched three TV shows.
5. He could score the winning run!

Underline the linking verb.

6. The twins are ten years old.
7. He looks tired, doesn't he?

Write *present, past,* or *future* to tell the tense of the underlined verb.

8. Josh <u>will play</u> this afternoon. _____
9. Susan <u>fell</u> down on the ice. _____
10. The squirrel <u>runs</u> up the tree. _____

**Answers:**

1. barks
2. threw
3. danced
4. have
5. could
6. are
7. looks
8. future
9. past
10. present

# Checkup 7

Name _____ Date _____

Complete each sentence with an action verb from the box.

1. Pedro _____ the other players carefully.

2. The giraffe _____ the leaves from the tree.

3. She always _____ the teacher questions.

| tears    asks    watched |

Circle the helping verb.

4. We could see the smoke from the fire.

5. The dancers are practicing their routines.

Underline the linking verb.

6. The students in the gym were loud.

7. My socks feel soft on my feet.

Write *present*, *past*, or *future* to tell the tense of the underlined verb.

8. We <u>see</u> whales swimming beside our boat. _____

9. They <u>will buy</u> a gift for her birthday party. _____

10. The apples <u>fell</u> off the tree yesterday. _____

Test A: Verbs

©The Education Center, Inc. • *Target Reading & Writing Success* • TEC60875 • Key p. 136

---

# Checkup 7

Name _____ Date _____

Complete each sentence with an action verb from the box.

1. Her sister _____ the flute in the marching band.

2. Eric _____ for his homework in his bookbag.

3. The player _____ the ball to tie the score.

| dunked    looked    plays |

Circle the helping verb.

4. He had tried to call you yesterday.

5. They could wait 15 minutes for a table.

Underline the linking verb.

6. The lion appears restless in his cage.

7. The girls were in their room.

Write *present*, *past*, or *future* to tell the tense of the underlined verb.

8. The singer <u>sang</u> my favorite song. _____

9. I <u>jump</u> higher than my brother. _____

10. We <u>will arrive</u> in half an hour. _____

Test B: Verbs

©The Education Center, Inc. • *Target Reading & Writing Success* • TEC60875 • Key p. 136

# It's Time to Take Aim!

On _____ our class will be having a checkup on **adjectives.**
To help your child prepare, please spend about 15 minutes reviewing this skill.

## Skill Refresher

Hide the answers at the bottom of the page. Guide your child through the rules and examples below. Then have him complete problems 1–14.

- Some adjectives **tell what kind.**

  | bright | silky | thirsty | green |
  |--------|-------|---------|-------|
  | lucky | cheerful | sour | wonderful |

- Some adjectives **tell how many.**

  | five | many | some | few |
  |------|------|------|-----|
  | more | twenty | several | nine |

- Adjectives can **compare** things.
  Add *-er* to compare two things.
  That boy is **taller** than me.
  Add *-est* to compare two or more things.
  Math is the **easiest** subject at school.

- If an adjective has three or more syllables, use **more/most** or **less/least** to show a comparison.

  | more difficult | most expensive |
  |----------------|----------------|
  | less dangerous | least important |

## Target These!

Circle the adjective and draw an arrow to the noun it describes.

1. gigantic house
2. soggy toast
3. steamy soup
4. several boxes

Circle each adjective that tells what kind.
Underline each adjective that tells how many.

5. playful dolphins
6. countless ants
7. crowded park
8. fifteen students
9. several cookies
10. sparkling car

Choose the correct adjective.

11. She was (hungry, hungrier, most hungry) than I was.
12. That book is the (good, better, best) book I've ever read.
13. Chili dogs are (delicious, more delicious, most delicious) than hamburgers.
14. My room is the (messy, more messy, messiest) room in the house.

**Answers:**

1. gigantic house
2. soggy toast
3. steamy soup
4. several boxes
5. playful dolphins
6. countless ants
7. crowded park
8. fifteen students
9. several cookies
10. sparkling car
11. hungrier
12. best
13. more delicious
14. messiest

©The Education Center, Inc. • *Target Reading & Writing Success* • TEC60875

# Checkup 8

Name _____ Date _____

Circle each adjective that tells what kind.
Underline each adjective that tells how many.

1. sparkling glass          4. loud room

2. bumpy field             5. few seedlings

3. some books              6. thirty-one answers

Circle the adjective(s) and draw an arrow to the noun that is described.

7. The neon sign was flashing.

8. We took a cruise on a huge ship.

9. I threw away the rusty bucket.

10. The candy was sticky.

11. Mike's old shoes are too tight.

12. The flowers were bright and fragrant.

Choose the correct adjective.

13. Mona wanted the (different, more different, most different) hat she could find.

14. The line is (slow, slower, slowest) than molasses.

15. The (helpful, more helpful, most helpful) salesperson worked with me.

---

# Checkup 8

Name _____ Date _____

Circle each adjective that tells what kind.
Underline each adjective that tells how many.

1. sharp pencil             4. several toppings

2. three books             5. pink pigs

3. scattered balls          6. many chances

Circle the adjective(s) and draw an arrow to the noun that is described.

7. I ran into a smelly goose.

8. This is a hungry puppy!

9. The goldfish is very active.

10. The park is too crowded.

11. The lights were bright and vivid.

12. I can't find a thing in Paul's messy closet!

Choose the correct adjective.

13. Peg chose the (small, more small, smallest) kitten.

14. Ted was always (serious, more serious, most serious) than Tad.

15. This is the (important, more important, most important) of the three tests.

# It's Time to Take Aim!

On _____ our class will be having a checkup on **adverbs**.
To help your child prepare, please spend about 15 minutes reviewing this skill.

## Skill Refresher

Hide the answers at the bottom of the page. Guide your child through the rules and examples below. Then have him complete problems 1–10.

- Some adverbs describe verbs. They tell **how, when,** or **where.**

  how: She whispered **quietly.**
  when: He rose **suddenly.**
  where: The students ran **outside.**

- Some adverbs describe adjectives. They tell **how.**
  This box is **too** heavy.

- Some adverbs describe adverbs. They tell **how** or **how much.**
  Max paints **very** carefully.

- Add *-er* or *-est,* use *more/most,* or use *less/least* to compare two or more things.
  Ben ran **faster** than I thought he would.
  Alice danced the **most gracefully** of all the dancers.

### Target These!

Circle each adverb and draw an arrow to the word it describes.

1. That wheel squeaks constantly.
2. Sue stepped inside.
3. Hanna sings beautifully.

Circle each adverb that tells how or how much.
Underline each adverb that tells when.
Draw a box around each adverb that tells where.

4. Ned eagerly bought the card.
5. We meet regularly.
6. Put the box anywhere.
7. Traffic moved very slowly.

Choose the correct adverb.

8. We got home (soon, sooner, soonest) than we thought.
9. Ed reached (wildly, more wildly, most wildly) for the net.
10. Sue sang the (loud, louder, loudest) of all.

---

**Answers:**

1. That wheel squeaks (constantly).
2. Sue stepped (inside).
3. Hanna sings (beautifully).
4. Ned (eagerly) bought the card.
5. We meet (regularly).
6. Put the box [anywhere].
7. Traffic moved (very) (slowly).
8. sooner
9. wildly
10. loudest

# Checkup 9

Name _____ Date _____

Circle each adverb. Draw an arrow to the word it describes.

1. The gem shone brightly.

2. Lynn gently held the lizard.

3. The movie ended too quickly.

4. Mom rather quietly calmed the baby.

Circle each adverb that tells how or how much. Underline each adverb that tells when. Draw a box around each adverb that tells where.

5. The dog is still hiding somewhere.

6. The snake smoothly slipped away.

7. Chad very calmly scrubbed the wall.

8. I often walk too slowly.

Choose the correct adverb.

9. I found the answer (easily, more easily, most easily).

10. The lily wilted (soon, sooner, soonest) of all the flowers.

11. Ty ate his cookie (slowly, more slowly, most slowly) than I did.

12. Jody put the box (high, higher, highest) than I can reach.

---

# Checkup 9

Name _____ Date _____

Circle each adverb. Draw an arrow to the word it describes.

1. Val sang the anthem well.

2. This punch is very sweet.

3. The parrot wildly flew around.

4. Ellen often hid things outside.

Circle each adverb that tells how or how much. Underline each adverb that tells when. Draw a box around each adverb that tells where.

5. Chris eagerly opened the letter.

6. Leo steadily climbed higher.

7. We eat pizza too often.

8. My pen's cap was really stuck, but I finally pushed it off.

Choose the correct adverb.

9. Will worked (steadily, more steadily, most steadily) than Ann did.

10. We watch TV (often, less often, least often) than we used to.

11. Toni has a (badly, worse, worst) sprained ankle.

12. Of all the climbers, Joe works the (hard, harder, hardest).

# It's Time to Take Aim!

On _____ our class will be having a checkup on **pronouns.**
To help your child prepare, please spend about 15 minutes reviewing this skill.

## Skill Refresher

Hide the answers at the bottom of the page. Guide your child through the rules and examples below. Then have him complete problems 1–8.

- A **pronoun** is a word that takes the place of a noun. Pronouns can be **singular** or **plural.**
  
  singular: I, me, my, mine, he, she, him, her, his, hers, it, its
  
  plural: we, us, our, ours, they, them, their, theirs
  
  both singular and plural: you, yours

- **Possessive pronouns** take the place of possessive nouns.
  
  The shoes belong to Paul. They are **his** shoes.

- Use the pronoun **I** as a subject. Use the pronoun **me** as a direct object.
  
  Sarah and **I** swim on Thursdays.
  
  My mom brings Sarah and **me** to swimming class.

- An **antecedent** is the noun that the pronoun replaces.
  
  **Shelly** said that **she** enjoyed the movie.

## Target These!

Write "S" for singular or "P" for plural.

1. her _____ its _____ they _____
2. theirs _____ him _____ yours _____

Complete each sentence using a possessive pronoun.

3. The car belongs to Mark. It is _____ car.
4. Carla's homework is late. _____ homework is late.

Complete each sentence using **I** or **me.**

5. Joshua and _____ are good friends.
6. The teacher saw Keisha and _____.

Circle the pronoun. Box its antecedent.

7. Max buried the bone and couldn't find it.
8. Wendy told her friend to call.

**Answers:**

1. S, S, P
2. P, S, S and P
3. his
4. Her
5. I
6. me
7. Max buried the [bone] and couldn't find (it)
8. [Wendy] told (her) friend to call.

# Checkup 10

Name _____ Date _____

Write "S" for singular or "P" for plural.

1. them _____   our _____   I _____

2. it _____   me _____   we _____

Complete each sentence using a possessive pronoun.

3. Paul's dog is Sparky. Sparky is _____ dog.

4. Those pencils belong to me. They are _____.

5. That is the girl's phone. It is _____.

Complete each sentence using *I* or *me*.

6. My mom told my sister and _____ to go to bed.

7. Last week, Baxter and _____ walked every day.

Circle the pronoun. Box its antecedent.

8. Carter told his brother about the game.

9. Mom and Dad bought themselves cars.

10. Carrie read Paul her favorite book.

**Test A:** Pronouns

---

# Checkup 10

Name _____ Date _____

Write "S" for singular or "P" for plural.

1. she _____   its _____   their _____

2. his _____   us _____   they _____

Complete each sentence using a possessive pronoun.

3. Katie's coat is in the closet. _____ coat is in the closet.

4. The team's picture is great! _____ picture is great.

5. The CD belongs to Will. It is _____.

Complete each sentence using *I* or *me*.

6. After school, Juan and _____ walked home.

7. My mom baked cookies for Eva and _____.

Circle the pronoun. Box its antecedent.

8. The cookies are warm and I love them!

9. The boy hurt himself on the playground.

10. Ian and Brett walked until they got tired.

**Test B:** Pronouns

# It's Time to Take Aim!

On _____ our class will be having a checkup on **sentences.**
To help your child prepare, please spend about 15 minutes reviewing this skill.

## Skill Refresher

Hide the answers at the bottom of the page. Guide your child through the rule and examples below. Then have him complete problems 1–9.

- Every sentence needs a **subject** and a **predicate** to express a complete thought. The subject names the person or thing spoken about, and the predicate tells something about the subject. A sentence can have a compound subject or a compound predicate.

  <u>Quentin and his team</u> <u>won the game.</u>
  subject          predicate

- A **simple sentence** is one complete thought. A **compound sentence** is two or more complete thoughts joined together by a conjunction and a comma.
  Simple sentence: We had dinner.
  Compound sentence: We had dinner, and we went dancing.

- **Fragments** are incomplete sentences. They are missing a subject, a verb, or a complete thought. A **run-on** is two or more simple sentences that run together without using the correct punctuation or a conjunction.
  Fragment: Saw them yesterday.
  Run-on: He danced too long his feet were hurting.

## Target These!

Circle the subject. Draw a box around the predicate.

1. Deon caught the ball.
2. Sarah baked and decorated the cake.

Write "simple" or "compound" to tell the type of sentence.

3. Sheila heard the thunder, and she ran inside. _____
4. Tony got a new puppy. _____

Write "fragment," "run-on," or "complete."

5. Eating dinner. _____
6. Pizza is my favorite food. _____
7. I like pepperoni the best I always order it. _____

On the back of this sheet, rewrite each fragment or run-on to make a complete sentence.

8. I thought the movie would never end I wanted to go home.
9. To the movies.

**Answers:**

1. [Deon] caught the ball.
2. (Sarah) baked and decorated the cake.
3. compound
4. simple
5. fragment
6. sentence
7. run-on
8. Answers will vary.
9. Answers will vary.

©The Education Center, Inc. • *Target Reading & Writing Success* • TEC60875

**122**

# Checkup 11

Name _____ Date _____

Circle the subject. Draw a box around the predicate.

1. Shelly and Kevin read the book.

2. We went shopping last Tuesday.

Write "simple" or "compound" to tell the type of sentence.

3. My parents and sisters gave me a new bike. _____

4. The elevator wasn't working, so we used the stairs. _____

Write "fragment," "run-on," or "sentence."

5. I'm going to the beach tomorrow. _____

6. Because I like. _____

7. I am staying for two weeks it will be fun. _____

Rewrite each fragment or run-on to make a complete sentence.

8. Tommy found.

_____

9. We went to the zoo we saw lots of animals.

_____

---

# Checkup 11

Name _____ Date _____

Circle the subject. Draw a box around the predicate.

1. I bought a new video game.

2. Peter and Mark borrowed it.

Write "simple" or "compound" to tell the type of sentence.

3. I found a quarter over there. _____

4. I changed my clothes and we went outside. _____

Write "fragment," "run-on," or "sentence."

5. I felt tired I had been cleaning my room all day. _____

6. Used all my spending money. _____

7. Danny made an A on his test. _____

Rewrite each fragment or run-on to make a complete sentence.

8. I ate tacos for lunch I ate chicken for dinner.

_____

9. Feeling happy.

_____

## Great aim!

_____
student

is right on target with

_____ !
skill

_____
teacher

_____
date

## You hit the bull's-eye!

_____
student

hit the mark with

_____ !
skill

_____
teacher

_____
date

1. anna conda loves living in the jungle.
2. She and bennie boa are best friends.
3. the two friends crawl along the riverbank and talk.
4. anna loves to watch mickey monkey swing from the branches.
5. mr. monkey's kids are afraid of anna.
6. it's no wonder the children are scared!
7. did you know anna can grow to be 30 feet long?
8. She is the longest snake in her village.
9. even though she sometimes bites, anna is not poisonous.
10. her teeth can cause bad wounds though.
11. when she gets hungry, anna wraps herself tightly around her dinner.
12. that's the time to stay out of anna's way!

1. One Flew Over the Moon
2. The View From Venus
3. A Star Is Born
4. The Man in the Moon

5. Galaxy Gazette
6. The Daily Star
7. The Space Observer
8. The Milky Way Press

9. "Twinkling Star"
10. "The Outer Limits of Space"
11. "Stargazing"

12. Space Quest
13. Mars Life
14. Eyes on Space

USE "SATEL-LIGHTS"

1. "Black Cat Strut"
2. "The Year of the Cat"
3. "The Cat From Outer Space"
4. "Wake Up, Wildcats!"
5. "A Dream of a Thousand Cats"
6. "Frisky Whiskers"
7. "Come Here, My Kitty"
8. "At the Scratching Post"

Answers for 9–13 will vary.

1. Bun E. Rabbit
   62 Barn House Trail
   Hareville, KY 20948

2. Ima Hare
   136 Carrot Place
   Rabbit Run, TX 58392

3. Fur E. Friend
   2800 Wabbit Way
   Bunny Hop, MA 38582

4. Pete R. Rabbit
   39 Hoppers Road
   Furville, NC 28764

5. Farmer Brown
   746 Barnyard Lane
   Hopping, SC 04952

6. Flop See
   291 Rabbit Hole Court
   Cotton Tail, TN 62522

| | Correct | Incorrect |
|---|---|---|
| 1. Dr. Woof sees patients on Monday, Tuesday, and Thursday. | E | A |
| 2. The doctor makes rounds at St. Bernard Hospital on Wednesday and Friday. | K | P |
| 3. Lane the Great Dane will have a checkup the last Friday in March. | L | S |
| 4. Sally Spaniel will come back in December to get her cast off. | M | D |
| 5. If Max Mutt is not well by Monday, Dr. Woof will put him in the hospital. | O | S |
| 6. Dr. Woof has seen 49 cats since Monday. | H | G |
| 7. Bobby Boxer visits the doctor every Thursday for a blood test. | E | C |
| 8. Dr. Woof is taking the month of June off to visit his family. | M | H |
| 9. Bonnie Beagle will need to take her medicine through next Sunday. | B | O |
| 10. Dr. Woof plays catch with his doctor friends on Saturdays. | F | L |
| 11. Tim Terrier will have surgery on the first Tuesday in May. | A | S |
| 12. Dr. Woof will check him the next Friday. | O | T |

"SHAM-POODLE"

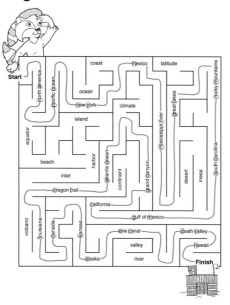

1. The largest city in the United States is New York City, sometimes called the Big Apple.
2. Many people move to the city from Puerto Rico, China, Central America, and the Caribbean Islands.
3. The Statue of Liberty stands on Liberty Island in New York Harbor.
4. New York City is divided into five boroughs: Manhattan, the Bronx, Queens, Brooklyn, and Staten Island.
5. Manhattan is surrounded by the Hudson River, the East River, the Harlem River, and Upper New York Bay.
6. One famous sight in New York City is the 102-story Empire State Building.
7. The World Trade Center's twin 110-story towers were once the tallest skyscrapers on Manhattan Island.

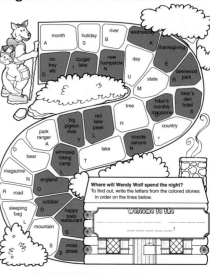

Where will Wendy Wolf spend the night?
To find out, write the letters from the colored stones in order on the lines below.

Welcome to the

OINKERS ONLY LODGE

1. Almost all fish are cold-blooded
2. Fish live in freshwater and salt water
3. Do all fish breathe through gills
4. Yes, they use their gills to breathe
5. How are fish and whales different
6. Whales are mammals
7. The smallest fish lives in the Indian Ocean
8. Did you know it's only one centimeter long
9. The largest fish weighs over 15 tons
10. Have fish been on Earth for 500 million years
11. Can fish survive in the Arctic
12. Yes, they can survive there

A FISH WITH A WISH

1. Sam, what are you doing?
2. I'm looking for all the food I stored last fall. I'm really hungry!
3. Do you remember where you hid it?
4. Well, I think I hid it near a pile of leaves. I just can't remember which one.
5. Do you want some help?
6. That would be great! Maybe if we both look we can find it.
7. Okay. I'll check these leaves near your nest.
8. I'll look over here by these bushes.
9. Do you see anything?
10. Not yet, but I'll keep looking.
11. I can hear my stomach growling. I hope we find it quickly!
12. Hey, Sam, I found your food!
13. Where was it?
14. It was right under your nose! It's in the leaves by your nest.

## Page 17

Exclamation mark answers will vary.
1. Which movie do you want to see?
2. Let's get tickets for *Going Bananas.*
3. Do you want some popcorn or candy?
4. I want some popcorn and a soda.
5. Here are the snacks.
6. Hurry up because the movie is starting!
7. Wow, this movie is fantastic!
8. I really like it too.
9. That jungle scene was awesome!
10. What do you think will happen next?
11. I think the monkey will chase the Banana Bandit.
12. Who will get the bananas in the end?
13. We'll just have to wait and see.
14. I love going to the movies!

## Page 18

Order of answers will vary.

| | |
|---|---|
| Boise, Idaho | March 26, 1988 |
| Miami, Florida | April 21, 1984 |
| Dallas, Texas | May 17, 1987 |
| Harrisburg, Pennsylvania | April 9, 1990 |
| Seattle, Washington | June 23, 1993 |
| Chicago, Illinois | July 15, 1998 |
| Boston, Massachusetts | October 8, 2000 |
| Bangor, Maine | December 28, 2001 |
| Phoenix, Arizona | February 18, 2003 |
| Baltimore, Maryland | April 3, 2004 |

## Page 19

**Guest List**

B Ima Bear
32 Shaggy Lane
New Orleans, LA 70112

L Grizzly Bear
142 Hibernating Lane
New York, NY 10001

K Wanna B. A. Bear
483 Rocky Mountain Road
Boise, ID 83701

U Bear E. Scary
947 Yellowstone Road
Jackson Hole, WY 83001

R Brown Bear
183 Hill Road
High Point, NC 27265

E Black E. Bear
P.O. Box 674
Grand Canyon, AZ 86023

B Poll R. Bear
P.O. Box 743
Nome, AK 99762

E Bay B. Bear
681 Furry Lane
New Bedford, MA 02740

Y Brown E. Bear
574 Cave Court
St. Paul, MN 55101

A Fuzzy Bear
283 Growling Lane
Lake Placid, NY 12946

R Furry Bear
563 Claw Court
Fort Lauderdale, FL 33301

Y Q. T. Bear
3526 Tree Lane
Libby, MT 59923

"BLUE-BEAR-Y"

## Page 20

Write the words for the camp letters in the correct order.
Add commas where needed.

Dear Mom,
Thanks for sending me to camp!
Can I come back again?
Love,
Sam

Dear Dad,
How can I get my roommate to stop snoring? Please write back soon.
Your sad son,
Steve

## Page 21

| Correct | Incorrect | | |
|---|---|---|---|
| E | F | 1. | Oh, I'm so glad you're serving lunch. |
| O | S | 2. | To keep it healthy, I'll order a salad. |
| H | M | 3. | Yes, I think I would like the soup too. |
| O | J | 4. | No, I don't need a straw for my water. |
| S | I | 5. | Waving wildly, Dino got the waitress's attention. |
| T | C | 6. | Excuse me, but I'd like to order some french fries too. |
| D | K | 7. | No, I think I'll have the baked potato instead. |
| O | A | 8. | After eating his soup and salad, Dino tried the potato. |
| E | A | 9. | After a bite, he realized the potato was cold. |
| R | I | 10. | Therefore, he sent the potato back to the kitchen. |
| R | B | 11. | Still, Dino wasn't full and ordered pie for dessert. |
| T | R | 12. | To satisfy Dino, the waitress brought him a huge piece of pie. |
| U | Z | 13. | Also, she refilled his water glass. |
| K | N | 14. | Wow, this key lime pie is tasty. |
| I | P | 15. | Yes, I think I will come back again! |

JURASSIC "PORK"

## Page 22

Sentences A, B, I, R, D, I, and E should be colored.

M I bought golf shoes, a hat, and a glove for the tournament.
O The prizes are cash, free golf lessons, and new clubs.
X Bring money for fees, a cart, and snacks.
S They take great care of the fairways, the cart paths, and the putting greens.
L Golf balls, tees, and towels are the pro shop's best sellers.
N I want a hamburger, french fries, and a cola from the snack bar.
H Should I use a driver, a wedge, or an 8-iron for this shot?
C I never hit a ball in the sand, lake, or trees.

A BIRDIE

## Page 23

Monday, November 8, 1684
The king and queen will be served turkey, mashed potatoes, and apple pie.

Tuesday, November 9, 1684
The king will get a snack platter with nuts, dates, pickles, and cooked apples.

Wednesday, November 10, 1684
Today is the queen's birthday! Her dinner will include salad, bean soup, and baked bananas.

Thursday, November 11, 1684
Prepare for the royal feast! The main course will be baked redfish, shrimp, lobster, and beef.

Friday, November 12, 1684
The king, the queen, and their friends will have tea this afternoon.

Saturday, November 13, 1684
The king wants only vegetables for today's dinner. We shall serve broccoli, red cabbage, and carrots.

Sunday, November 14, 1684
It's time to feed the king's sweet tooth with mints, muffins, tarts, and hot cocoa.

Monday, November 15, 1684
Lady Dara will visit today! A meal will include spicy sausage, custard, and apple cider.

Tuesday, November 16, 1684
The king and queen will ask for their favorite breakfast, lunch, and dinner.

39 Missing Commas

## Page 24

123 Meadow Road
Mouseville, WI 00001
June 14, 2004

Ms. Callie Cowley, Manager
The Cheese Factory
4200 Cheesy Avenue
Cheddar, WI 00002

Dear Ms. Cowley:

I am writing to ask for your help. My friends Mark, Maddie, Mary, and I are having a cheese-tasting contest. We are trying to see who can taste the most types of cheese in two weeks. I am in second place right now. I have tried 12 different types of cheese. My favorites are Swiss, cheddar, and Colby.

I was hoping you could send me some samples of your cheese. I would like to try Gouda, Muenster, Edam, and blue. Should I pay you with cash, a check, or a money order?

Sincerely,
Mike Mouse

## Page 25

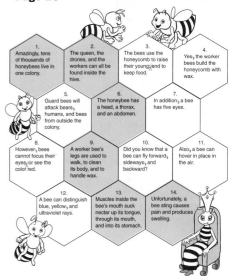

1. Amazingly, tens of thousands of honeybees live in one colony.
2. The queen, the drones, and the workers can all be found inside the hive.
3. The bees use the honeycomb to raise their young, and to keep food.
4. Yes, the worker bees build the honeycomb with wax.
5. Guard bees will attack bears, humans, and bees from outside the colony.
6. The honeybee has a head, a thorax, and an abdomen.
7. In addition, a bee has five eyes.
8. However, bees cannot focus their eyes, or see the color red.
9. A worker bee's legs are used to walk, to clean its body, and to handle wax.
10. Did you know that a bee can fly forward, sideways, and backward?
11. Also, a bee can hover in place in the air.
12. A bee can distinguish blue, yellow, and ultraviolet rays.
13. Muscles inside the bee's mouth suck nectar up its tongue, through its mouth, and into its stomach.
14. Unfortunately, a bee sting causes pain and produces swelling.

## Page 26

Sentences 2, 4, 5, 7, and 9 should be colored red.

1. Everyone, be sure to read the instructions.
3. Watch out for that wet paint, Paco.
6. Sketch your drawing in pencil first, Pam.
8. Polly, you'll need to let the paint dry first.
10. Pat, look at the painting I just finished.

## Page 27

1. Our teacher, <u>Mrs. Finley,</u> loves to teach grammar.
2. Mackie Reel, <u>the smartest kid in school,</u> won the spelling bee.
3. He spelled *hippopotamus*, <u>the hardest word in his category.</u>
4. Today I have <u>smoked sardines,</u> my favorite lunch.
5. Barry Cuda, <u>my best friend,</u> sits next to me in math class.
6. We are making small floats and masks for Mardi Gras, <u>a festival.</u>
7. We learned about oceanography, <u>a part of geography which includes oceans, seas, and marine life.</u>
8. Our school football team, <u>the Fighting Fins,</u> won the game.
9. I tried out for the lead role in *Five Fishy Friends*, <u>the school play.</u>
10. My class is going on a field trip to Aquatic World, <u>the new aquarium.</u>
11. My science fair project, <u>Exploring the World's Oceans,</u> won first prize.
12. Today we read *Three Fish in the Ocean*, <u>my favorite book.</u>
13. Bea Fish, <u>a children's author,</u> is visiting our school next week.
14. I have homework in math and reading, <u>my two favorite subjects.</u>
15. Tomorrow is Friday, <u>the best day of the week!</u>

## Page 28

Sentences 2, 3, 5, 8, and 12 should be colored.

1. The Daisy family, original from Texas, loves sunshine.
4. It was 78 degrees yesterday, Dena.
6. Dana, the tallest flower, grew two inches in three days.
7. Did you see that dragonfly, Damon?
9. Delia, the youngest flower, likes to play in the rain.
10. Donny, that's the most colorful butterfly I've ever seen.
11. The Daisy's friends, the Roses, live next door.

## Page 29

| | yes | no |
|---|---|---|
| 1. How far have we traveled?" asked Fran." | X | O |
| 2. "We've gone about 130 miles," answered Fred. | D | R |
| 3. "The car is sounding a bit strange," replied Fran. | T | P |
| 4. Don't "worry, said" Fred. | S | I |
| 5. "The car just stopped! exclaimed" Fran. | Q | Z |
| 6. "Let me see," said Fred, "if I can fix this." | F | B |
| 7. "What do you think it is? asked Fran. | C | A |
| 8. "Watch out! yelled Fran. The radiator is steaming!" | V | K |
| 9. "Thanks for the warning," answered Fred. | E | M |
| 10. "Then Fran shouted, "Be careful! Don't stand too close to the road. | N | H |
| 11. "I know," answered Fred. "Those cars are zooming by." | G | W |
| 12. With a sigh, Fred said, "I don't think I can fix this." | L | J |

HE HAD IT "TOAD" OFF

## Page 30

1. Sighing, Bob said, "It's been a long day on the trail."
2. "I feel like I've been eating dust all day," grumbled Arnie.
3. "You should've worn a bandanna like me," said Lou with a grin.
4. Arnie rubbed his belly and said, "I think I'll cook some chili."
5. "I need a few more logs for the campfire," called Arnie.
6. Bob and Lou moaned and said, "Oh, we'll go and get some."
7. "Keep an eye out for coyotes!" exclaimed Arnie. "I heard one howl."
8. "Is supper ready yet? I'm hungry!" whined Lou.
9. "I smell something good!" yelled Bob.
10. "Is it our supper?" asked Lou.
11. "It is," answered Arnie. "Let's eat!"
12. Bob laughed and said, "I'd rather eat chili than dust any day!"

Answers will vary for 13, 14, and 15.

## Page 31

1. Al the announcer roared, "It's a grand day for Tiger baseball!"
2. "It's a warm, sunny day," he said.
3. Fanny asked, "What time does the game start?"
4. The crowd cheered, "Go Tigers! Go Tigers!"
5. "Hot dogs! Sodas! Cotton candy!" yelled Vinny the vendor.
6. Coach Growly told his team, "We need to play hard today!"
7. The umpire called, "Batter up!"
8. "Hit a homer, Tim!" yelled Fanny.
9. "I'll take three hot dogs with extra chili," Fred told Vinny.
10. The umpire shouted, "Foul ball!"
11. "Heads up, fans. Here comes a fly ball!" Al shouted.
12. Vinny shouted, "That almost hit me!"
13. "Did you see that ball sail out of the park?" Fanny asked.
14. "Get up for the seventh-inning stretch," Al announced.
15. "The game's over," Al howled. "The Tigers win!"

## Page 32

C — The radio blared, "Get tip-top service at Fletcher's Garage!"

G — Fletcher asked, "What's wrong with your truck, Mr. Yota?"

A — "The horn doesn't work," Troy Yota told Fletcher.

E — "I can't get my car into first gear!" blurted Sue Barroo.

H — Fletcher said, "I need to test-drive your car, Sue."

F — Cora Vet cut in and said, "My car's brake pedal squeaks."

D — "Would you check the fuel filter too?" Cora asked.

B — Fletcher told Cora, "Your car needs a tune-up."

## Page 33

| Direct | Indirect | |
|---|---|---|
| O | U | 1. Coach Kay said, "Let's practice making jump shots." |
| E | N | 2. Coach Kay said that we need to work on our layups. |
| P | S | 3. "Get the ball and face the basket!" Coach Kay shouted. |
| G | I | 4. "Coach Kirby will help us out this week," said Coach Kay. |
| O | M | 5. Coach Kirby said that he'll teach us how to dunk! |
| J | B | 6. "Split up into two groups," Coach Kay said. |
| C | F | 7. Coach Kay said that he'd take the first group. |
| W | R | 8. Coach Kay said, "I'm going to teach you to jump-stop." |
| K | T | 9. "Jump," said Coach Kay. "Then catch the ball and land." |
| A | G | 10. Coach Kirby said that Coach Kay used to be his coach. |
| C | L | 11. He said, "I'll teach you how to dribble behind your backs." |
| P | H | 12. "Right now," Coach Kirby stated, "let's work on jump balls." |
| D | J | 13. Coach Kirby said that it takes timing to get a jump ball. |
| V | Y | 14. "Okay, let's switch groups!" yelled Coach Kay. |
| G | X | 15. Coach Kirby said, "Now I'll teach you how to dunk!" |

BECAUSE THEY DRIBBLE

## Page 34

Sentences 1, 2, 6, 8, 10, and 11 should be colored brown.

3. "Hurry up," Ivan said, "and don't forget to bring your money."
4. "What'll you have?" Ike asked.
5. "I'd like a rocky road ice-cream cone with two scoops," Ira replied.
7. "I'll have a chocolate chip ice-cream sandwich," Ira chimed in.
9. "Do you have rainbow ice pops?" Ivan asked.
12. "We'll be waiting!" everyone yelled.

## Page 35

1. Tina asked, "Hey, Tammy, are you ready to run?"
2. "It's so early," Tammy groaned.
3. "Why don't we warm up a little first?" Tammy asked.
4. Tina suggested, "Let's walk for a couple of minutes to warm up."
5. Tammy said, "Okay. I think I'm ready."
6. "There's a 5K race next month," Tina commented.
7. "A 5K race!" Tammy exclaimed. "How many miles are in a 5K race?"
8. "It's only 3.1 miles," Tina explained.
9. "We run two miles every day," Tina continued.
10. "Two long miles," Tammy grumbled.
11. "Come on," Tina begged. "It will be fun!"
12. Tina chanted, "We're going to run in a 5K race."
13. "Shhh, I'm training," muttered Tammy.
14. "I'm training to run my first 5K race," Tammy said with a smile.

## Page 36

All jewels should be colored.

1. Captain Claw said, "(T)he sky looks dark and gloomy."
2. "(W)e'll never make it to the island," Feathers groaned.
3. Feathers whined, "(T)he ship's rocking is making me sick."
4. The crew begged, "(C)aptain, can we please turn back?"
5. "(N)o!" bellowed the captain. "(W)e will find the treasure."
6. "(L)ook!" squawked Redbeard. "(T)here is land ahead!"
7. Blue Beak climbed the mast and declared, "(A)hoy! He's right!"
8. "(I)t will be our pleasure," Feathers sang, "to find the hidden treasure."
9. "(T)he waves are dying down," Captain Claw noted.
10. The captain ordered, "(G)et close to the sandy beach."
11. "(A)ye, aye, Captain," Blue Beak whistled with a salute.
12. Feathers called, "(L)ast one off the ship is a rotten bird!"
13. "(L)ook there," Blue Beak called. "(I)s that the treasure chest?"
14. "(I)t is!" Redbeard shouted. "(W)e're rich!"

## Page 37

The following sentence numbers should be circled: 1, 3, 6, 7

The sentences below should be corrected as shown.

2. "**Y**ou want breakfast already**?**" April asked**.**
4. "**O**kay," whinnied Morgan, "I'll just have oats again**.**"
5. "**P**a wants us to move some hay," April told Morgan.
8. "**A**w, it's your turn," April said. "I drove last week**.**"
9. "Well, are you ready to go?" asked Morgan.
10. "No," fussed April, "I still have to eat!"

## Page 38

The sentences below should be corrected as shown.

3. Pat read a poem called **"**Ode to a Comb**"** out loud.
4. Paul said it made him think about **"**Pretty Prickly,**"** his favorite song.
7. **"**The Hokey-Pokey,**"** the song Pat liked best, came on the radio.
8. Paul said he loved the song **"**Comb, Comb, Comb Your Quill.**"**
10. Paul said he loved its theme song, **"**Think Pink.**"**
11. Pat asked if the song came from the poem **"**When I Think of You.**"**
12. Pat turned to **"**Quick Quill Curls**"** and read the article to Paul.
14. Paul said **"**This Is Me**"** is the title of the book's first chapter.

Hint: Use **quotation marks** around the titles of poems, articles, songs, and book chapters. **Underline** book, magazine, and movie titles.

## Page 39

| | | |
|---|---|---|
| ballerina**'s** slippers | person**'s** cleats | salesperson**'s** shoe polish |
| shopper**'s** boots | owner**'s** flats | buyer**'s** flip-flops |
| mother**'s** clogs | brother**'s** sneakers | clerk**'s** shoes |
| father**'s** loafers | child**'s** socks | sister**'s** sandals |

## Page 40

The following sentence numbers should be colored: 2, 4, 6, 8, 12, 13.

The sentences below should be corrected as shown.

1. This year**'s** vacation for the Penguin family was at the beach.
3. Pete and his brothers saw many animals**'** homes on the beach.
5. They they noticed some sea turtles**'** nests.
7. The sea star**'s** skin looked bumpy and rough.
9. The dunes**'** tall grasses made it hard to see the ball.
10. The boys found the ball, and then they saw dolphins**'** fins in the water.
11. The dolphins were playing with a friend**'s** Frisbee disks.
14. The next day, the Penguin family went sailing in two neighbors**'** boats.
15. Everyone agreed this was the Penguin**'s** best trip ever!

## Page 41

M. Look at all these ___clothes___ ! (clothes, clothes')
T. My favorite ___outfits___ are red and orange. (outfits, outfits')
S. Those ___girls'___ shoes are neat. (girls, girls')
L. I'll put those ___sweaters___ back on their hangers. (sweaters, sweaters')
N. Both ___shirts'___ colors are too dull. (shirts, shirts')
V. Look! These ___belts___ are on sale! (belts, belts')
O. I would love to have two ___pairs___ of pants. (pairs, pairs')
A. All the ___pants'___ legs are too long for me. (pants, pants')
I. Let's each try on one of those ___dresses___ ! (dresses, dresses')
K. The ___dresses'___ styles look great on you! (dresses, dresses')
E. Both ___shirts'___ sizes are too small. (shirts, shirts')
R. The ___hats'___ bows match the dresses perfectly. (hats, hats')
W. What ___items___ are you going to buy? (items, items')
G. I think I'll get two ___hats___ and a dress. (hats, hats')
S. The ___items'___ total cost is $43.36. (items, items')

"SNAKERS"

## Page 42

1. horses' reins
2. groomer's brush
3. horses' stables
4. owners' saddles
5. horse's food
6. horses' stalls
7. horse's bridle
8. ranches' trails
9. horses' hooves
10. horses' manes
11. horse's horseshoes
12. riders' blankets
13. horses' hay
14. rider's trophy
15. horses' corral

LITTLE "COLT"

## Page 43

1. Both teams' best bowler**X**s are going first.
2. The player**X**s' shirts are green.
3. Steve's team has blue bowling balls.
4. Where are the first bowler**X**s shoes?
5. The shoes are in each player's bag.
6. The first two bowler**X**s' scores were 234 and 268.
7. The Super Strikers' average score is 273.
8. Their star player's score is 296.
9. Now it is the Bayside Bowlers' turn.
10. Knock M. Down's first ball went into the gutter.
11. The player's second ball was a strike!
12. Now the teams' scores are almost even.
13. It is Steve Strike's turn to bowl.
14. This player**X**s scores are always the highest.
15. Steve's team has won the championship!

## Page 44

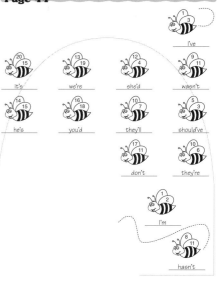

| | | | |
|---|---|---|---|
| 20 / 15 — it's | 13 / 15 — we're | 12 / 4 — she'd | 9 / 11 — wasn't |
| 14 / 7 — he's | 16 / 18 — you'd | 10 / 7 — they'll | 5 / 3 — should've |
| 17 / 11 — don't | 18 — | 10 / 6 — they're | |

1 / 3 / I've

1 / 2 / I'm

8 / 11 / hasn't

hasn't

## Page 45

1. here's
2. she'll
3. he's
4. you're
5. they'll
6. wouldn't
7. who's
8. should've
9. she's
10. weren't
11. what is or what has
12. she had or she would
13. was not
14. there is or there has
15. there will
16. we have
17. have not
18. he will

## Page 46

1. Dan Chers, Monday, two thirty-five, 2:35 — I
2. S. Miles, Monday, seven fifty-eight, 7:58 — A
3. B. R. Aces, Monday, eight thirty, 8:30 — T
4. Phil A. Tooth, Monday, twelve fifteen, 12:15 — F
5. Anita Crown, Tuesday, eleven forty-five, 11:45 — R
6. E. Namel, Tuesday, two fifty, 2:50 — T
7. Floss Yurteeth, Wednesday, four twenty, 4:20 — T
8. Nomar Cavity, Wednesday, ten forty, 10:40 — H
9. Mo Larr, Thursday, three ten, 3:10 — Y
10. B. I. Cuspid, Thursday, six fifty-five, 6:55 — O
11. Eva Brushin, Friday, three twenty-five, 3:25 — T
12. Phil Ling, Friday, one forty-five, 1:45 — T
13. N. O. Sugar, Wednesday, ten twenty, 10:20 — I
14. Pearl E. White, Monday, four twenty-five, 4:25 — E
15. Willy Grin, Friday, ten thirty, 10:30 — R

**What's the best time to visit the dentist?**

To solve the riddle, match the circled letters to the numbered lines below.

A F T E R "T O O T H - I R T Y I"
7:58 12:15 2:50 4:25 10:40   8:30 6:55 11:45 1:45 4:20   2:35 10:30 3:25 3:10 10:20

## Page 47

1. These days might be good for a beach picnic: Friday, Sunday, or Monday.
2. We could invite four friends: Olive, Otis, Opal, and Oscar.
3. Last time, we had too much junk food: chips, cookies, and candy.
4. This time, let's bring healthier snacks like these: fruit, nuts, or cheese.
5. We can grill the following: burgers, hot dogs, and corn.
6. Let's bring these drinks: water, fruit juice, and soda.
7. We'll need these paper products: plates, napkins, and cups.
8. Otis can bring this gear: a kite, a beachball, and a football.
9. We can play these games: flag football, tag, and catch.
10. We always buy two things at the beach: ice cream and sun screen.

## Page 48

Dr. Ceros will speak about two types of rhinos: the black rhino and the white rhino.
Monday at 7:00 P.M.

Dr. Ceros will talk about what rhinos eat: grass, leafy twigs, and shrubs.
Tuesday at 10:00 A.M.

Learn about these rhino traits: horns, thick skin, and three-toed feet.
Monday at 11:00 A.M.

Watch a film about where wild rhinos roam: Africa and Asia.
Monday at 6:00 P.M.
Thursday at 10:00 A.M.

Dr. Ceros will sign copies of his latest books: *The Rhino's Plant-Eating Pals* and *The Rhino's Meat-Eating Neighbors.*
Saturday from 2:30 P.M. until 4:00 P.M.

Sign up at any of these shops: Student Central, Book Inn, or Readers Corner.

## Page 49

| | |
|---|---|
| E | O |
| T | S |
| I | T |
| O | N |
| N | E |
| U | C |
| L | H |
| E | T |
| O | B |
| D | G |
| F | E |
| H | S |

ON THE OUTSIDE

## Page 50

1. I have to be at school early (by 7:15) Friday.
2. I'm going to the Student Writing Crew (SWC) meeting.
3. I'll be writing the meeting's minutes (report of what happened).
4. The last meeting (two weeks ago) lasted for one hour.
5. This week's meeting should be half as long (30 minutes).
6. Ms. Penny (the SWC sponsor) said there are two new writing contests.
7. I am going to enter the Have Pencil Will Travel (HPWT) writing contest.
8. The Putting It on Paper Company (PIPC) is having a contest too.
9. If you want to enter, call their toll-free number (1-555-667-2797).
10. The Write and Refine Group (WRG) helps sponsor the SWC.

"MY, YOU LOOK SHARP TONIGHT!"

## Page 53

Common Nouns: basketball, name, friend, fans, baskets, games, players, article, referees
Proper Nouns: Sheila, Dribblers, Robin, Raleigh, Coach Net, *Athletes Today,* Charlotte, Star Arena, Monday

## Page 54

1. shells
2. beaches
3. child
4. fish
5. glass
6. wave
7. shovels
8. man
9. foot
10. sodas
11. leaves
12. lunch
13. boxes
14. teeth
15. radios
16. flies

## Page 55

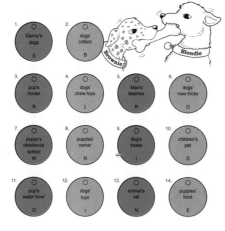

BLONDIE

## Page 56

## Page 57

1. Mike, Meredith, and I (were) fishing one day.
2. We were hoping each of us (would) catch a fish.
3. I wondered if I (could) sit on the boat long enough.
4. Suddenly, something (was) pulling on Meredith's line!
5. We thought we (would) see a huge fish!
6. The weight of the fish (was) bending the fishing pole.
7. Meredith (was) grasping the fishing pole tightly.
8. We told her she (should) reel it in quickly.
9. Remember that a large fish (can) pull you off a boat.
10. All three of us (were) trying to pull in the fish.
11. Suddenly, we (were) looking at Meredith's giant fish.
12. Instead of a fish, Meredith (had) caught a whale!
13. Who (would) believe us?
14. Three minnows (had) caught a huge whale!
15. You (should) tell this story to your friends!

## Page 58

1. looks
2. smells
3. grew
4. sounds
5. seemed
6. remained
7. became
8. were
9. The crowd grew very excited as the band played.
10. Larry and Luke were happy to be invited.
11. This new music sounds perfect for dancing.
12. Liz looks fantastic in her new dance outfit.
13. Lisa became a dancer when she was four years old.
14. Lisa seemed sad when the dance was over.
15. Lulu remained friends with her dance partner.